1A

FOUR CORNERS

Second Edition | Student's Book
with Digital Pack

JACK C. RICHARDS & DAVID BOHLKE

CAMBRIDGE

Shaftesbury Road, Cambridge CB2 8EA, United Kingdom

One Liberty Plaza, 20th Floor, New York, NY 10006, USA

477 Williamstown Road, Port Melbourne, VIC 3207, Australia

314–321, 3rd Floor, Plot 3, Splendor Forum, Jasola District Centre, New Delhi – 110025, India

103 Penang Road, #05–06/07, Visioncrest Commercial, Singapore 238467

Cambridge University Press & Assessment is a department of the University of Cambridge.

We share the University's mission to contribute to society through the pursuit of education, learning and research at the highest international levels of excellence.

www.cambridge.org
Information on this title: www.cambridge.org/9781009286107

© Cambridge University Press & Assessment 2012, 2019, 2023

First published 2012
Second edition 2019

20 19 18 17 16 15 14 13

Printed in Poland by Opolgraf

A catalogue record for this publication is available from the British Library

ISBN 978-1-009-28597-1   Student's Book with Digital Pack 1
ISBN 978-1-009-28610-7   Student's Book with Digital Pack 1A
ISBN 978-1-009-28598-8   Student's Book with Digital Pack 1B
ISBN 978-1-108-63367-3   Teacher's Edition with Complete Assessment Program 1
ISBN 978-1-009-28599-5   Full Contact with Digital Pack 1
ISBN 978-1-009-28600-8   Full Contact with Digital Pack 1A
ISBN 978-1-009-28616-9   Full Contact with Digital Pack 1B
ISBN 978-1-009-28593-3   Presentation Plus Level 1

Additional resources for this publication at www.cambridge.org/fourcorners

Authors' acknowledgments

Many people contributed to the development of *Four Corners*. The authors and publisher would like to particularly thank the following **reviewers**:

Nele Noe, **Academy for Educational Development, Qatar Independent Secondary School for Girls**, Doha, Qatar; Pablo Stucchi, **Antonio Raimondi School** and **Instituto San Ignacio de Loyola**, Lima, Peru; Nadeen Katz, **Asia University**, Tokyo, Japan; Tim Vandenhoek, **Asia University**, Tokyo, Japan; Celso Frade and Sonia Maria Baccari de Godoy, **Associação Alumni**, São Paulo, Brazil; Rosane Bandeira, **Atlanta Idiomas**, Manaus, Brazil; Cacilda Reis da Silva, **Atlanta Idiomas**, Manaus, Brazil; Gretta Sicsu, **Atlanta Idiomas**, Manaus, Brazil; Naila Maria Cañiso Ferreira, **Atlanta Idiomas**, Manaus, Brazil; Hothnã Moraes de Souza Neto, **Atlanta Idiomas**, Manaus, Brazil; Jacqueline Kurtzious, **Atlanta Idiomas**, Manaus, Brazil; José Menezes Ribeiro Neto, **Atlanta Idiomas**, Manaus, Brazil; Sheila Ribeiro Cordeiro, **Atlanta Idiomas**, Manaus, Brazil; Juliana Fernandes, **Atlanta Idiomas**, Manaus, Brazil; Aline Alexandrina da Silva, **Atlanta Idiomas**, Manaus, Brazil; Kari Miller, **Binational Center**, Quito, Ecuador; Alex K. Oliveira, **Boston University**, Boston, MA, USA; Noriko Furuya, **Bunka Gakuen University**, Tokyo, Japan; Robert Hickling, **Bunka Gakuen University**, Tokyo, Japan; John D. Owen, **Bunka Gakuen University**, Tokyo, Japan; Elisabeth Blom, **Casa Thomas Jefferson**, Brasília, Brazil; Lucilena Oliveira Andrade, **Centro Cultural Brasil Estados Unidos (CCBEU Belém)**, Belém, Brazil; Marcelo Franco Borges, **Centro Cultural Brasil Estados Unidos (CCBEU Belém)**, Belém, Brazil; Geysa de Azevedo Moreira, **Centro Cultural Brasil Estados Unidos (CCBEU Belém)**, Belém, Brazil; Anderson Felipe Barbosa Negrão, **Centro Cultural Brasil Estados Unidos (CCBEU Belém)**, Belém, Brazil; Henry Grant, **CCBEU – Campinas**, Campinas, Brazil; Maria do Rosário, **CCBEU – Franca**, Franca, Brazil; Ane Cibele Palma, **CCBEU Inter Americano**, Curitiba, Brazil; Elen Flavia Penques da Costa, **Centro de Cultura Idiomas – Taubaté**, Taubaté, Brazil; Inara Lúcia Castillo Couto, **CEL LEP – São Paulo**, São Paulo, Brazil; Sonia Patricia Cardoso, **Centro de Idiomas Universidad Manuela Beltrán**, Barrio Cedritos, Colombia; Geraldine Itiago Losada, **Centro Universitario Grupo Sol (Musali)**, Mexico City, Mexico; Nick Hilmers, **DePaul University**, Chicago, IL, USA; Monica L. Montemayor Menchaca, **EDIMSA**, Metepec, Mexico; Angela Whitby, **Edu-Idiomas Language School**, Cholula, Puebla, Mexico; Mary Segovia, **El Monte Rosemead Adult School**, Rosemead, CA, USA; Dr. Deborah Aldred, **ELS Language Centers, Middle East Region**, Abu Dhabi, United Arab Emirates; Leslie Lott, **Embassy CES**, Ft. Lauderdale, FL, USA; M. Martha Lengeling, **Escuela de Idiomas**, Guanajuato, Mexico; Pablo Frias, **Escuela de Idiomas UNAPEC**, Santo Domingo, Dominican Republic; Tracy Vanderhoek, **ESL Language Center**, Toronto, Canada; Kris Vicca and Michael McCollister, **Feng Chia University**, Taichung, Taiwan; Flávia Patricia do Nascimento Martins, **First Idiomas**, Sorocaba, Brazil; Andrea Taylor, **Florida State University in Panama**, Panamá, Panama; Carlos Lizárraga González, **Grupo Educativo Angloamericano**, Mexico City, Mexico; Bo-Kyung Lee, **Hankuk University of Foreign Studies**, Seoul, South Korea; Dr. Martin Endley, **Hanyang University**, Seoul, South Korea; Mauro Luiz Pinheiro, **IBEU Ceará**, Ceará, Brazil; Ana Lúcia da Costa Maia de Almeida, **IBEU Copacabana**, Copacabana, Brazil; Maristela Silva, **ICBEU Manaus**, Manaus, Brazil; Magaly Mendes Lemos, **ICBEU São José dos Campos**, São José dos Campos, Brazil; Augusto Pelligrini Filho, **ICBEU São Luis**, São Luis, Brazil; Leonardo Mercado, **ICPNA**, Lima, Peru; Lucia Rangel Lugo, **Instituto Tecnológico de San Luis Potosí**, San Luis Potosí, Mexico; Maria Guadalupe Hernández Lozada, **Instituto Tecnológico de Tlalnepantla**, Tlalnepantla de Baz, Mexico; Karen Stewart, **International House Veracruz**, Veracruz, Mexico; Tom David, **Japan College of Foreign Languages**, Tokyo, Japan; Andy Burki, **Korea University, International Foreign Language School**, Seoul, South Korea; Jinseo Noh, **Kwangwoon University**, Seoul, South Korea; Neil Donachey, **La Salle Junior and Senior High School**, Kagoshima, Japan; Rich Hollingworth, **La Salle Junior and Senior High School**, Kagoshima, Japan; Quentin Kum, **La Salle Junior and Senior High School**, Kagoshima, Japan; Geoff Oliver, **La Salle Junior and Senior High School**, Kagoshima, Japan; Martin Williams, **La Salle Junior and Senior High School**, Kagoshima, Japan; Nadezhda Nazarenko, **Lone Star College**, Houston, TX, USA; Carolyn Ho, **Lone Star College-Cy-Fair**, Cypress, TX, USA; Kaoru Kuwajima, **Meijo University**, Nagoya, Japan; Alice Ya-fen Chou, **National Taiwan University of Science and Technology**, Taipei, Taiwan; Raymond Dreyer, **Northern Essex Community College**, Lawrence, MA, USA; Mary Keter Terzian Megale, **One Way Línguas-Suzano**, São Paulo, Brazil; B. Greg Dunne, **Osaka Shoin Women's University**, Higashi-Osaka, Japan; Robert Maran, **Osaka Shoin Women's University**, Higashi-Osaka, Japan; Bonnie Cheeseman, **Pasadena Community College** and **UCLA American Language Center**, Los Angeles, CA, USA; Simon Banha, **Phil Young's English School**, Curitiba, Brazil; Oh Jun Il, **Pukyong National University**, Busan, South Korea; Carmen Gehrke, **Quatrum English Schools**, Porto Alegre, Brazil; John Duplice, **Rikkyo University**, Tokyo, Japan; Wilzania da Silva Nascimento, **Senac**, Manaus, Brazil; Miva Silva Kingston, **Senac**, Manaus, Brazil; Lais Lima, **Senac**, Manaus, Brazil; Mengjiao Wu, **Shanghai Maritime University**, Shanghai, China; Wen hsiang Su, **Shih Chien University Kaohsiung Campus**, Kaohsiung, Taiwan; Yuan-hsun Chuang, **Soo Chow University**, Taipei, Taiwan; Lynne Kim, **Sun Moon University (Institute for Language Education)**, Cheon An City, Chung Nam, South Korea; Regina Ramalho, **Talken English School**, Curitiba, Brazil; Tatiana Mendonça, **Talken English School**, Curitiba, Brazil; Ricardo Todeschini, **Talken English School**, Curitiba, Brazil; Monica Carvalho da Rocha, **Talken English School**, Joinville, Brazil; Karina Schoene, **Talken English School**, Joinville, Brazil; Diaña Peña Munoz and Zira Kuri, **The Anglo**, Mexico City, Mexico; Christopher Modell, **Tokai University**, Tokyo, Japan; Song-won Kim, **TTI (Teacher's Training Institute)**, Seoul, South Korea; Nancy Alarcón, **UNAM FES Zaragoza Language Center**, Mexico City, Mexico; Laura Emilia Fierro López, **Universidad Autónoma de Baja California**, Mexicali, Mexico; María del Rocío Domínguez Gaona, **Universidad Autónoma de Baja California**, Tijuana, Mexico; Saul Santos Garcia, **Universidad Autónoma de Nayarit**, Nayarit, Mexico; Christian Meléndez, **Universidad Católica de El Salvador**, San Salvador, El Salvador; Irasema Mora Pablo, **Universidad de Guanajuato**, Guanajuato, Mexico; Alberto Peto, **Universidad de Oaxaca**, Tehuantepec, Mexico; Carolina Rodriguez Beltan, **Universidad Manuela Beltrán, Centro Colombo Americano**, and **Universidad Jorge Tadeo Lozano**, Bogotá, Colombia; Nidia Milena Molina Rodriguez, **Universidad Manuela Beltrán** and **Universidad Militar Nueva Granada**, Bogotá, Colombia; Yolima Perez Arias, **Universidad Nacional de Colombia**, Bogotá, Colombia; Héctor Vázquez García, **Universidad Nacional Autónoma de Mexico**, Mexico City, Mexico; Pilar Barrera, **Universidad Técnica de Ambato**, Ambato, Ecuador; Deborah Hulston, **University of Regina**, Regina, Canada; Rebecca J. Shelton, **Valparaiso University, Interlink Language Center**, Valparaiso, IN, USA; Tae Lee, **Yonsei University**, Seodaemun-gu, Seoul, South Korea; Claudia Thereza Nascimento Mendes, **York Language Institute**, Rio de Janeiro, Brazil; Jamila Jenny Hakam, **ELT Consultant**, Muscat, Oman; Stephanie Smith, **ELT Consultant**, Austin, TX, USA.

Scope and sequence

LEVEL 1	Learning outcomes	Grammar	Vocabulary
Welcome Unit Pages 2–3 **Classroom language** Page 4	Students can ... ☑ introduce themselves and others ☑ say hello and good-bye		
Unit 1 Pages 5–14			
New friends A *What's your name?* B *How do you spell it?* C *Are you a student?* D *Names and jobs*	Students can ... ☑ ask for and say names ☑ spell names ☑ talk about where people are from and what they do ☑ discuss people's names and jobs	The verb *be* Possessive adjectives Subject pronouns *Yes / no* questions with *be*	Names and titles Interesting jobs
Unit 2 Pages 15–24			
People and places A *Where are you from?* B *What's your email address?* C *Family* D *Family and friends*	Students can ... ☑ ask for and say people's nationalities ☑ ask for and give phone numbers and email addresses ☑ identify family members and give their ages ☑ give information about family and friends	Plural subject pronouns Questions with *be* *Who* and *How old* with *be*	Nationalities Family members Numbers 0–101
Unit 3 Pages 25–34			
What's that? A *Is this your notebook?* B *What's this called in English?* C *Clothing* D *Favorite things*	Students can ... ☑ ask about and identify everyday items ☑ ask what something is called in English ☑ talk about clothes and possessions ☑ describe favorite possessions	Demonstratives Articles *a* and *an* Plurals Possessive pronouns *Whose* *'s* and *s'*	Everyday items Clothes and colors
Unit 4 Pages 35–44			
Daily life A *Getting around* B *What time is it?* C *My routine* D *My weekend*	Students can ... ☑ describe how people get around ☑ ask for and tell the time ☑ ask and answer questions about routines ☑ describe the things they do on weekends	Simple present statements Simple present *yes / no* questions	Ways of getting around Days of the week and routines
Unit 5 Pages 45–54			
Free time A *Online habits* B *How much is it?* C *What do you do for fun?* D *Online fun*	Students can ... ☑ talk about their online habits ☑ accept and decline help ☑ ask and answer questions about leisure activities ☑ discuss how they use technology	Adverbs of frequency Simple present *Wh-* questions with *do*	Online activities Leisure activities and places
Unit 6 Pages 55–64			
Work and play A *What does she do?* B *Can I speak to ... ?* C *Can you sing?* D *Work and study*	Students can ... ☑ identify and talk about jobs ☑ ask for someone on the telephone ☑ have someone wait ☑ describe their talents and abilities ☑ talk about study and work programs	Simple present *Wh-* questions with *does* *Can* for ability *And, but,* and *or*	Jobs Abilities

Functional language	Listening and Pronunciation	Reading and Writing	Speaking
Interactions: Saying hello Saying good-bye			• Introductions • Greetings
Interactions: Asking for spelling	**Listening:** Spelling names **Pronunciation:** Contractions	**Reading:** "Famous Names" An article **Writing:** My name	• Class introductions and greetings • *Keep talking*: Name circle • Class name list • Guessing game about famous people • *Keep talking*: "Find the differences" activity about jobs and cities • Quiz about celebrities
Interactions: Asking for someone's phone number Asking for someone's email address	**Listening:** Directory Assistance calls Information forms People I know **Pronunciation:** Word stress	**Reading:** "People in My Life" Photo captions **Writing:** My friends	• True and false information about people • *Keep talking*: Interviews with new identities • Class survey for new contact information • Information exchange about family members • *Keep talking*: Family trees • Presentation about friends
Interactions: Asking what something is	**Listening:** Things around the classroom Favorite things **Pronunciation:** Plurals	**Reading:** "Yuna's Blog: My favorite things!" A blog post **Writing:** My favorite thing	• Questions and answers about personal items • *Keep talking*: Things in the closet • Memory game about everyday items • Personal items and their owners • *Keep talking*: "Find the differences" activity about clothing colors • Presentation of favorite things
Interactions: Asking the time	**Listening:** Times of different events Angela's routine **Pronunciation:** Reduction of *to*	**Reading:** "What's your favorite day of the week?" A message board **Writing:** About my weekend	• Survey about getting to school and work • *Keep talking*: Transportation facts • Interview about the times of specific events • Interview about routines • *Keep talking*: "Find someone who" activities about routines • Survey about busy weekends
Interactions: Declining help Accepting help	**Listening:** Shopping Favorite websites **Pronunciation:** Thirteen or thirty?	**Reading:** "Fun Online Activities" An article **Writing:** Let's chat	• Comparison of online habits • *Keep talking*: Interview about online habits • Role play of a shopping situation • Interview about leisure activities • *Keep talking*: Interviews about fun activities • Discussion about favorite websites
Interactions: Asking for someone on the phone Having someone wait	**Listening:** Telephone calls Ads for overseas programs **Pronunciation:** *Can* and *can't*	**Reading:** "Fun Jobs" An article **Writing:** My abilities	• "Find someone who" activity about jobs • *Keep talking*: Memory game about jobs • Role play of a phone call • Interview about abilities • *Keep talking*: Board game about abilities • Discussion about study and work programs

Welcome

1 Introducing yourself

A 🎧 Listen and practice.

> **Simon** Hello. I'm Simon.
> **Chen** Hi, Simon. My name is Chen. Nice to meet you.
> **Simon** Nice to meet you, too.

B **PAIR WORK** Introduce yourselves.

2 Introducing someone else

A 🎧 Listen and practice.

> **Simon** Chen, this is my friend Sofia.
> **Sofia** Hi, Chen. Nice to meet you.
> **Chen** Nice to meet you, too, Sofia.

B **GROUP WORK** Introduce your partner from Exercise 1 to another classmate.

3 Hi and bye

A 🎧 Listen and practice.

Simon Hi, Chen!
Chen Good morning, Simon! How are you?
Simon I'm fine, thanks. And you?
Chen Fine, thank you.

Simon See you later, Chen!
Chen Bye, Simon!

B 🎧 Listen to the expressions. Then practice the conversation again with the new expressions.

Saying hello
Hi.
Hello.
Good morning.
Good afternoon.
Good evening.

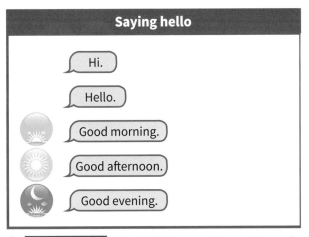

Saying good-bye
Bye.
Good-bye.
See you.
See you later.
See you tomorrow.

C CLASS ACTIVITY Say hello to your classmates and ask how they are. Then say good-bye.

I can introduce myself and others. ✅
I can say hello and good-bye. ✅

3

Classroom language

Pair work

Group work

Class activity

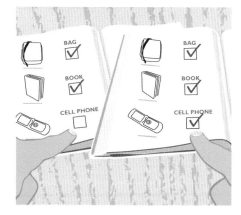

Compare answers.

Cover the picture.

Go to page 12.

Ask and answer questions.

Interview your partner.

Role-play the situation.

1 New friends

☐ Noah   ☐ Sophia

☐ Michael   ☐ James   ☐ Harper

Warm Up

Popular names in the United States

A Check (✓) the popular names.

B Say ten popular names in your country.

5

A What's your name?

1 Language in context First day of class

🎧 Listen to Ms. Peters meet her students on the first day of class. <u>Underline</u> the names.

2 Vocabulary Names and titles

A 🎧 Listen and repeat.

first name   middle name   last / family name

Jennifer Ann Wilson
full name

Miss Gomez = a single woman

Mrs. Chow = a married woman

Ms. Peters = a single or married woman

Mr. Adams = a single or married man

B **PAIR WORK** Complete the sentences with your own information. Then compare answers.

My first name is _____.

My family name is _____.

My full name is _____.

My teacher's name is _____.

3 Grammar 🎧 The verb *be*; possessive adjectives

What is (**What's**)	your name?	**My** name **is** Maria.
	his name?	**His** name **is** Ricardo.
	her name?	**Her** name **is** Yoko.
What are	your names?	**Our** names **are** Maria and Jason.
	their names?	**Their** names **are** Ricardo and Yoko.

A Circle the correct words. Then compare with a partner.

1 Maria is a student. **His** / **Her** last name is Gomez.

2 Ms. Peters **is** / **are** our teacher. **Her** / **Their** first name is Linda.

3 My name is Jason. What's **our** / **your** name?

4 Anna and Bruce **is** / **are** students. **Her** / **Their** teacher is Miss Brown.

5 Their first names **is** / **are** Yoko and Ricardo.

6 Hello, everyone. I'm Miss Diaz. What are **your** / **his** names?

B Complete the conversation with the correct words. Then practice in a group.

A Hello. Welcome to English class.

What ___is___ your name, please?

B _____ name is Pam.

A And what's _____ last name, Pam?

B My last name _____ Nelson.

A OK. And _____ is *your* name?

C Ji-ah. _____ family name is Lee.

4 Speaking My name is ...

A **CLASS ACTIVITY** Meet your classmates. Say your first and last name.

A: Hello. My name is Oscar Martinez. What's your name?

B: Hi. My name is Susana Harris.

A: It's nice to meet you.

B: Nice to meet you, too.

B Share your information.

A: What's his name?

B: His name is Oscar Martinez. What's her name?

A: Sorry, I don't know.

5 Keep talking!

Go to page 125 for more practice.

I can ask for and say names. ✓

B How do you spell it?

1 The alphabet

A 🎧 Listen and repeat.

A	B	C	D	E	F	G	H	I	J	K	L	M

N	O	P	Q	R	S	T	U	V	W	X	Y	Z

B **PAIR WORK** Say a letter. Your partner points to it. Take turns.

2 Interactions Spelling names

A 🎧 Listen and practice.

Donald	Hello. My name is Donald Wang.
Clerk	How do you spell your first name?
Donald	D-O-N-A-L-D.
Clerk	And how do you spell your last name?
Donald	W-A-N-G.

Asking for spelling

How do you spell your first name?   How do you spell your last name?

B **PAIR WORK** Practice the conversation again with these names.

John Evans	Cindy Douglas	Antonia Lopez	Richard Wu

A: Hello. My name is John Evans.

B: Hello, John. How do you spell your first name?

A: J-O-H-N.

B: And how do you spell . . . ?

3 Listening Spell it!

A 🎧 Listen to four people spell their names. Check (✓) the correct answers.

1 ✓ Steven 2 ☐ Dina 3 ☐ Kelly 4 ☐ Bryan
☐ Stephen ☐ Dena ☐ Kerry ☐ Brian

B 🎧 Listen to the conversations. Write the names.

H E L L O.
My name is

George _____.

1

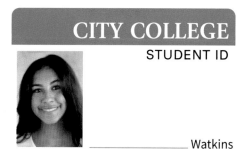

CITY COLLEGE
STUDENT ID

_____ Watkins

2

10:00 English Class

1. _____ _____

3

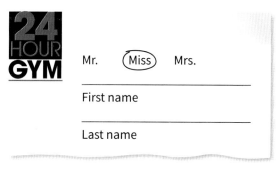

24 HOUR GYM

Mr. (Miss) Mrs.
_____
First name
_____
Last name

4

File Edit View Favorites Tools Help

Back x Search Favorites Media

Address Go

First name: Paul
Middle name:
Last name:

5

Welcome, students!
Ms._____

6

4 Speaking A class list

CLASS ACTIVITY Ask your classmates for their names. Make a list.

A: What's your first name?
B: Tyler.
A: How do you spell it?
B: T-Y-L-E-R.
A: And what's your last name?
B: Larsen.

First names	Last names
Tyler	Larsen
Lindsey	Fisher
Marcela	Perez
Evan	Howley
Dmitri	Benos

I can spell names. ✓

C Are you a student?

1 Vocabulary Interesting jobs

A 🎧 Listen and repeat.

Salma Hayek is an **actress**.
She's from Mexico.

Tadanobu Asano is an **actor**.
He's from Japan.

Alex Hornest is an **artist**.
He's from Brazil.

Kendall Jenner is a **model**.
She's from the United States.

Lang Lang is a **musician**.
He's from China.

Rihanna is a **singer**.
She's from Barbados.

B PAIR WORK Name other people for each job.

A: Jet Li is an actor.

B: Yes. And Meryl Streep is an actress.

2 Conversation My friend the musician

🎧 Listen and practice.

Sandy	Hey, Jacob!
Jacob	Oh, hi, Sandy. How's it going?
Sandy	Good, thanks. This is my friend Kevin.
Jacob	Hi. Nice to meet you.
Kevin	Nice to meet you, Jacob.
Jacob	Are you a student here?
Kevin	No, I'm not. I'm a musician.
Sandy	Kevin is from England.
Jacob	Oh? Are you from London?
Kevin	No, I'm not. I'm from Liverpool.

3 Grammar 🎧 Subject pronouns; *yes* / *no* questions with *be*

I'm a musician.	**Am I** in your class?
	Yes, **you are**. No, **you're not**. / No, **you aren't**.
You're a student.	**Are you** from London?
	Yes, **I am**. No, **I'm not**.
Kevin **is** from Liverpool.	**Is he** a singer?
He's from Liverpool.	Yes, **he is**. No, **he's not**. / No, **he isn't**.
Sandy **is** a student.	**Is she** from Canada?
She's a student.	Yes, **she is**. No, **she's not**. / No, **she isn't**.
Liverpool **is** in England.	**Is your** name John?
It's in England.	Yes, **it is**. No, **it's not**. / No, **it isn't**.

Contractions I'm = I am   you're = you are   he's = he is   she's = she is   it's = it is

A Match the questions and the answers. Then practice with a partner.

1 Is your first name Jacob? ___d___
2 Are you from Liverpool? _____
3 Is she from the United States? _____
4 Is she a musician? _____
5 Is Will Smith an actor? _____
6 Is Quito in Peru? _____

a No, I'm not. I'm from London.
b Yes, he is. He's a singer, too.
c No, she's not. She's an artist.
d Yes, it is. And my last name is King.
e No, it's not. It's in Ecuador.
f Yes, she is. She's from California.

B Complete the conversations with the correct words. Then practice with a partner.

1 A ___Is___ your first name Don?
   B No, _____ not. It's Jeff.
2 A _____ you from Mexico?
   B Yes, I _____. I'm from Mexico City.
3 A _____ your teacher from England?
   B No, she _____.
4 A _____ you a model?
   B No, _____ not. I'm a singer.

4 Pronunciation Contractions

🎧 Listen and repeat. Notice the reduction of contractions.

I am → I'm   he is → he's   it is → it's   are not → aren't

you are → you're   she is → she's   is not → isn't

5 Speaking Ten questions

GROUP WORK Think of a famous person with a job from Exercise 1. Your group asks ten questions and guesses the name. Take turns.

A: Is the person a man?
B: No, she's not.
C: Is she an actress?

6 Keep talking!

Student A go to page 126 and Student B go to page 128 for more practice.

I can talk about where people are from and what they do. ✓

D Names and Jobs

1 Reading 🎧

A Look at the pictures. What are their names?

B Read the article. Are they all singers?

FAMOUS NAMES

Actor **Tom Cruise** uses his middle name as his last name. His full name is Thomas Cruise Mapother. Tom is short for Thomas.

Zhang Ziyi is an actress from China. Zhang isn't her first name. It's her family name. In China, family names come first.

Shakira is a singer from Colombia. She uses only her first name. Her full name is Shakira Isabel Mebarak Ripoll.

Jay-Z is a hip-hop singer from the United States. Jay-Z is his nickname. His real name is Shawn Corey Carter.

Pelé is a soccer player from Brazil. His full name is Edson Arantes do Nascimento. Pelé is his nickname.

Madonna is not a nickname for this singer. It's her first name. Her full name is Madonna Louise Veronica Ciccone.

C Read the article again. Complete the sentences with the correct words.

1 Tom Cruise uses his _____middle_____ name as his last name.

2 Shakira uses only her _____ name.

3 Edson Arantes do Nascimento's _____ is Pelé.

4 Ziyi is not Zhang Ziyi's _____ name.

5 Jay-Z's _____ name is Shawn Corey Carter.

6 Madonna Louise Veronica Ciccone is Madonna's _____ name.

D PAIR WORK Tell your partner about another famous person's name.

"Rain is a singer, actor, and model from South Korea. Rain is his nickname. His real name is Jeong Ji-hoon."

2 **Writing** My name

A Write sentences about your name. Use the model to help you.

> **My Name**
>
> My full name is Anthony Steven Johnson. My nickname is Big Tony. Tony is short for Anthony. My middle name is Steven, and my last name is Johnson.

B GROUP WORK Tell your group about your name.

3 **Speaking** Celebrity quiz

A PAIR WORK Ask and answer the questions about celebrities.

1 She's an actress from the U.K. Her initials are E. W. What's her name?

"Her name is Emma Watson."

2 She's an actress from Colombia. Her last name is Vergara. What's her first name?

3 He's a soccer player from Argentina. His first name is Lionel. What's his last name?

4 She's an actress and singer. Her nickname is J-Lo. What's her name?

5 He's an actor from Australia. His first name is Hugh. What's his last name?

6 She's an actress from the United States. Her last name is Lawrence. What's her first name?

B PAIR WORK Create a quiz. Write three sentences about a celebrity.

He's a basketball player.
He's from the United States.
His first name is LeBron.

C GROUP WORK Say your sentences to another pair. They guess the celebrity. Take turns.

A: He's a soccer player.
B: Is he Neymar?
A: No, he isn't. He's from Portugal.

Wrap-up

1 Quick pair review

Lesson A Do you remember?

What are your classmates' last names? Answer with the information you remember.
You have two minutes.

A: Her last name is Fernandes.

B: Yes, it is. And his first name is Oscar. What's his last name?

A: It's Medina.

Lesson B Test your partner!

Say your full name. Can your partner write it correctly? Check his or her answer.
You have two minutes.

First name	Middle name	Last / Family name
_____	_____	_____

Lesson C Brainstorm!

Make a list of interesting jobs. How many do you know? You have one minute.

Lesson D Guess!

Describe your favorite celebrity, but don't say his or her name! Can your partner
guess the name? Take turns. You have two minutes.

A: He's a singer and a musician. He's from the United States. He's in Maroon 5.

B: Is he Adam Levine?

A: Yes!

2 In the real world

What is your favorite movie? Go online and find information in English about
five actors or actresses in the movie. Then write about them.

- What are their names?
- Where are they from?

Actors in "The Avengers"

My favorite movie is "The Avengers."
Chris Hemsworth is an actor in the movie.
He's from Australia ...

2 People and places

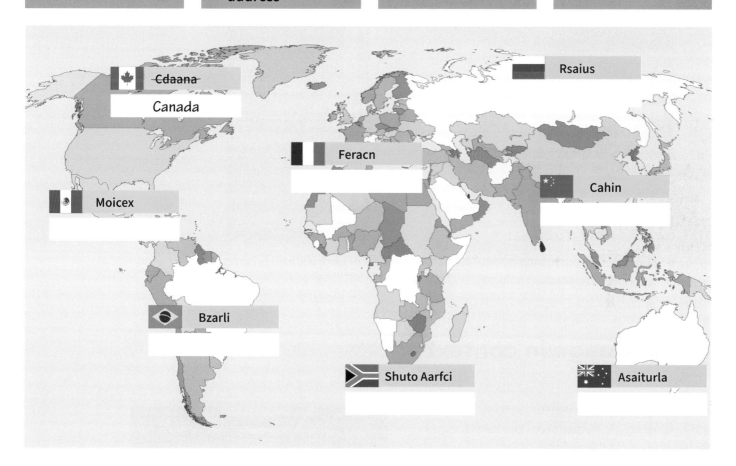

Rsaius

~~Cdaana~~
Canada

Feracn

Cahin

Moicex

Bzarli

Shuto Aarfci

Asaiturla

Warm Up

A Write the names of the countries.

B Say the names of five other countries in English.

A Where are you from?

1 Vocabulary Nationalities

A 🎧 Complete the chart with the correct nationalities. Then listen and check your answers.

Mexican	American	South Korean	Chilean	Greek	Colombian
Spanish	Canadian	Brazilian	Saudi	Peruvian	Japanese
British	Chinese	Turkish	Thai	Ecuadorian	✓ Australian

Country		Nationality	Country		Nationality
	Australia	Australian		Japan	
	Brazil			Mexico	
	Britain			Peru	
	Canada			Saudi Arabia	
	Chile			South Korea	
	China			Spain	
	Colombia			Thailand	
	Ecuador			Turkey	
	Greece			The United States	

B **PAIR WORK** Say a famous name. Your partner says his or her nationality. Take turns.

A: Mark Zuckerberg.

B: He's from the United States. He's American.

2 Language in context New neighbors

🎧 Listen to Brad and Emily Hill talk about their new neighbors. What are their names?

Brad	Who are they?
Emily	Oh, they're our new neighbors, Carlos and Claudia.
Brad	Are they musicians?
Emily	Yes, they are.
Brad	Where are they from?
Emily	They're from Brazil.
Brad	What city are they from?
Emily	They're from Manaus.

3 Grammar 🎧 Plural subject pronouns; questions with *be*

Where are you and Sakura from?
    We're from Japan.
 	
What city are **you** from?
    We're from Osaka.
 	
Are you Japanese?
    Yes, **we are.**
    No, **we're not.** / No, **we aren't.**
	Where are Carlos and Claudia from?
	    They're from Brazil.
	
	What city are **they** from?
	    They're from Manaus.
	
	Are they Brazilian?
	    Yes, **they are.**
	    No, **they're not.** / No, **they aren't.**

Contractions   we're = we are   they're = they are

Complete the conversations with the correct words. Then practice with a partner.

1   A   Where are _____you_____ from?

    B   We're from Mexico.

    A   Oh? _____ city are you from? Are you from Mexico City?

    B   No, we _____ not. _____ from Monterrey.

2   A   _____ Jim and Carly American?

    B   No, they _____. They _____ Canadian.

    A   What city in Canada are _____ from?

    B   They _____ from Toronto.

4 Pronunciation Word stress

A 🎧 **Listen and repeat. Notice the stressed syllables in the nationalities.**

●	●•	•●•	•●
Greek	**Bri**tish	Bra**zil**ian	Chi**nese**

B 🎧 **Listen and repeat. Underline the stressed syllables in the nationalities.**

Japa<u>nese</u>   Australian   Spanish   Thai

5 Speaking That's not correct!

A   **Write three false sentences about people, countries, or nationalities.**

   1. Rio de Janeiro and São Paulo are in Portugal.

   2. Beyoncé and Solange are British.

   3. Kate and Pippa Middleton are Australian.

B   **GROUP WORK**   **Share your sentences. Your group corrects them. Take turns.**

   A: Rio de Janeiro and São Paulo are in Portugal.

   B: No, they aren't. They're in Brazil.

6 Keep talking!

Go to page 127 for more practice.

I can ask for and say people's nationalities.   ✓   17

B What's your email address?

1 Numbers 0 to 10; phone numbers; email addresses

A 🎧 Listen and repeat.

0	1	2	3	4	5	6	7	8	9	10
zero	one	two	three	four	five	six	seven	eight	nine	ten

B 🎧 Listen and repeat. Notice that people sometimes say "oh" for "zero" in phone numbers.

281-363-2301 = "two-eight-one, three-six-three, two-three-zero-one"

602-374-4188 = "six-oh-two, three-seven-four, four-one-eight-eight"

C 🎧 Listen and repeat. Notice the way people say email addresses.

susan8k@cup.org = "susan-eight-K-at-C-U-P-dot-org"

jun_akita@email.com = "jun-underscore-akita-at-email-dot-com"

2 Interactions Phone numbers and email addresses

A 🎧 Listen and practice.

Stacy	Hey, Emma. What's your phone number?
Emma	It's 309-403-8708.
Stacy	What's your email address?
Emma	It's emma@cup.org.
Stacy	Thanks!

B 🎧 Listen to the expressions. Then practice the conversation again with the new expressions.

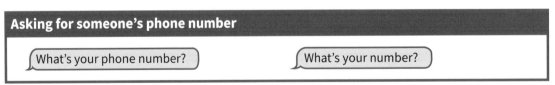

Asking for someone's phone number

What's your phone number?   What's your number?

Asking for someone's email address

What's your email address?   What's your email?

C **PAIR WORK** Practice the conversation again with the information below.

978-887-8045   ej5@cup.org

604-608-4864   emma_jones@email.com

3 Listening What name, please?

A 🎧 Listen to four people call Directory Assistance for phone numbers.
Check (✓) the correct answers.

1 Carlos Moreno ☐ 333-822-1607 ✓ 323-822-1607
2 Lucy Chang ☐ 662-651-0410 ☐ 662-615-0410
3 Michael Ashcroft ☐ 866-279-9400 ☐ 866-279-9500
4 Beatriz J. Lago ☐ 341-360-7450 ☐ 341-360-4570

B 🎧 Listen to three people give their names, phone numbers, and email addresses.
Complete the forms.

MADISON ENGLISH SCHOOL
REGISTRATION

First name: _Michael_
Middle name: _John_
Last name: _____
Phone: _____
Email: _____

1-2-3 GYM
MEMBERSHIP

First name: _____
Middle initial: _P._
Last name: _____
Phone: _____
Email: _____

CityLibrary
CARD APPLICATION

First name: _____
Family name: _____
City: _Dallas_
Phone: _____
Email: _____

4 Speaking A new number and email address

A Write a new phone number and email address.

My new phone number: _____   My new email address: _____

B **CLASS ACTIVITY** Ask five classmates for their names, new phone numbers, and
new email addresses. Complete the chart with their answers.

	Name	Phone number	Email address
1			
2			
3			
4			
5			

C Share your information.

A: What's her name and phone number?
B: Her name is Fatima. Her phone number is 212-691-3239.
A: What's her email address?
B: Her email is ...

I can ask for and give phone numbers and email addresses. ✓

C Family

1 Vocabulary Family members

A 🎧 Listen and repeat.

grandparents
grandfather Roger Mills
grandmother Sarah Mills
parents
father (dad) Michael Olson
mother (mom) Helen Olson
children / kids

husband
wife

son
daughter

sister Wendy Olson
brother Jack Olson
brother Brian Olson

B **PAIR WORK** Ask and answer the questions about the family in Part A.

1 Are Sarah and Roger Mills single?
2 Are Michael and Helen brother and sister?
3 Are Sarah and Roger grandparents?
4 Are Wendy and Jack parents?

2 Conversation Who's that?

🎧 Listen and practice.

Lance   Who's that?
Jack   That's my sister. Her name is Wendy.
Lance   How old is she?
Jack   She's seven.
Lance   Is she your only sister?
Jack   Yeah.
Lance   And who are they?
Jack   They're my grandparents.
Lance   Wow. They look young.
         And who's he?
Jack   That's me!

3 Grammar 🎧 *Who* and *How Old* with *be*

Who's that?	Who are they?
That's my sister.	They're my grandparents.
How old is she?	How old are they?
She's seven (years old).	They're 70 and 66.

11 eleven
12 twelve
13 thirteen
14 fourteen
15 fifteen
16 sixteen
17 seventeen
18 eighteen
19 nineteen
20 twenty
21 twenty-one
22 twenty-two
23 twenty-three
24 twenty-four
25 twenty-five
26 twenty-six
27 twenty-seven
28 twenty-eight
29 twenty-nine
30 thirty
40 forty
50 fifty
60 sixty
70 seventy
80 eighty
90 ninety
100 one hundred
101 one hundred (and) one

A Read the answers. Write the questions. Then practice with a partner.

A   Who's that?

B   Oh, that's my brother Ignacio.

A   _____

B   He's ten years old.

A   _____

B   They're my sisters Lucia, Antonia, and Carmen.

A   _____

B   They're 19, 16, and 11.

A   And _____

B   That's my grandfather.

A   _____

B   He's 62.

B PAIR WORK Ask and answer questions about the family in Exercise 1.

A: Who's that?

B: That's Jack Olson.

4 Speaking My family

A Complete the chart with information about three people in your family.

	Family member	Name	How old ... ?	Where ... from?
1				
2				
3				

B PAIR WORK Tell your partner about your family. Ask and answer questions for more information.

A: Keiko is my grandmother. She's 73.

B: Where is she from?

5 Keep talking!

Go to page 129 for more practice.

I can identify family members and give their ages. ✓

D Family and friends

1 Reading 🎧

A Look at the people in Isabel's photos. Who are they? Guess.

B Read the photo descriptions. Who are Isabel's family members? Who are her friends?

PEOPLE IN MY LIFE

I'm with my friends Fernando and Amy. Fernando is on the left. He's from Bogotá, Colombia. Amy is on the right. She's from Perth, Australia. I'm in the middle.

This is my brother Carlos and my sister Julia. Carlos is 18 years old and a good soccer player. Julia is only ten. She's a good tennis player.

This is my grandmother. Her name is Olivia, but her nickname is Nana. She's an artist, and she's 92 years old!

Here's my Internet friend Dong-sun. His family name is Choi. He's from Busan, South Korea. He's 18 years old. His sister is in the photo, too.

C Read the photo descriptions again. Correct the false sentences.

1 Isabel and Amy are ~~sisters~~.   Isabel and Amy are friends.

2 Carlos isn't a good soccer player.   _____

3 Olivia is 90 years old.   _____

4 Isabel and Dong-sun are classmates. _____

D **PAIR WORK** Ask and answer the questions about Isabel's family and friends.

- Who are Fernando and Amy?
- What's Olivia's nickname?
- How old is Julia?
- What city is Dong-sun from?

2 Listening People I know

A 🎧 Listen to Gina show some photos to her friend. Who are the people?
Check (✓) the correct answers.

1 ☐ friend
☑ brother

2 ☐ classmate
☐ sister

3 ☐ father
☐ grandfather

4 ☐ teacher
☐ mother

B 🎧 Listen again. Answer the questions.

1 How old is Mark? _____15_____

2 What city is Dominique from? _____

3 What's the man's name? _____

4 Is Ms. Parker American? _____

3 Writing and speaking My friends

A Complete the chart with information about three friends. Then find photos or
draw pictures of them.

	Friend 1	Friend 2	Friend 3
Name			
Age			
Nationality			
Other information			

B Write sentences about your friends in the pictures. Use the
model and your answers in Part A to help you.

My friends

My best friend is Samantha. She's 26 years old.

She's American. She's a teacher.

Emma is my friend, too. She's …

C **GROUP WORK** Share your pictures and sentences. Ask and answer questions
for more information.

A: This is my friend Samantha. She's 26 years old.

B: What's her last name?

Wrap-up

1 Quick pair review

Lesson A Guess!

Say five countries. Can your partner name the nationalities? Take turns.
You have two minutes.

A: South Korea.

B: South Korean.

Lesson B Test your partner!

Write three phone numbers and say them to your partner. Can your partner
write them correctly? Check his or her answers. You have two minutes.

My phone numbers	My partner's phone numbers
_____	_____
_____	_____
_____	_____

Lesson C Brainstorm!

Make a list of family words. How many do you know? You have one minute.

Lesson D Find out!

Are any of your friends or family members from the same cities? You have
two minutes.

A: My father is from Mexico City, and my mother is from Guadalajara.

B: My grandmother is from Guadalajara, too!

2 In the real world

Go online and find information in English about a country from another part
of the world. Then write about it.

- What are five cities in the country?
- What are the names and ages of two famous people
  from the country?

South Korean Cities and People

Seoul, Busan, Incheon, Daegu, and Ulsan are five

cities in South Korea. Daniel Dae Kim is a famous

actor from Busan, South Korea. He's ...

Busan

3 What's that?

LESSON A
- Everyday items
- Demonstratives; articles *a* and *an*; plurals

LESSON B
- Asking what something is

LESSON C
- Clothes and colors
- Possessive pronouns; *Whose*; *'s* and *s'*

LESSON D
- Reading: "Yuna's Blog: My favorite things!"
- Writing: My favorite thing

Year: ___1969___

Year: _____

Year: _____

Year: _____

Warm Up

A Label the pictures with the correct years.

| ✓ 1969 | 1995 | 1978 | 1986 |

B Can you name five things in the pictures?

A Is this your notebook?

1 Vocabulary Everyday items

A 🎧 Listen and repeat.

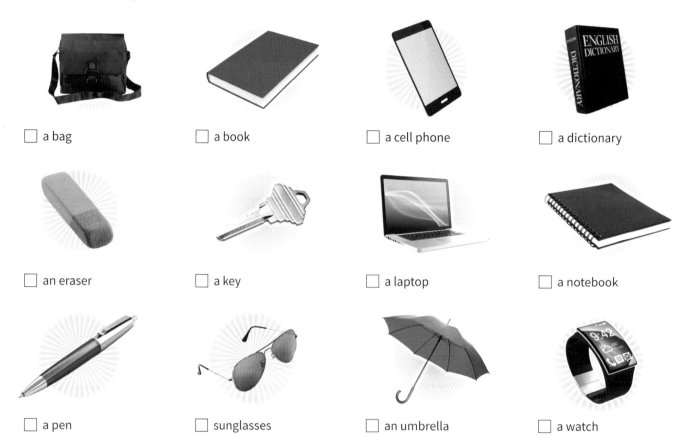

☐ a bag ☐ a book ☐ a cell phone ☐ a dictionary

☐ an eraser ☐ a key ☐ a laptop ☐ a notebook

☐ a pen ☐ sunglasses ☐ an umbrella ☐ a watch

B Check (✓) the things in your classroom. Then compare answers.

2 Language in context What are those?

🎧 Listen to four people talk about everyday items. Circle the items in the conversations.

Pete	Hey, Ling. What's that?
Ling	Oh, it's my watch.
Pete	It's nice. What are those?
Ling	They're my English books.

Susie	Are these your sunglasses?
Pablo	No, they're not.
Susie	Is this your notebook?
Pablo	Yes, it is. Thanks.

3 Grammar 🎧 Demonstratives; articles *a* and *an*; plurals

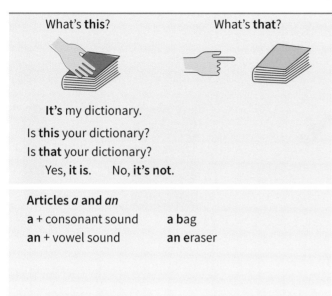

What's **this**?   What's **that**?

It's my dictionary.

Is **this** your dictionary?
Is **that** your dictionary?
    Yes, **it is**.   No, **it's not**.

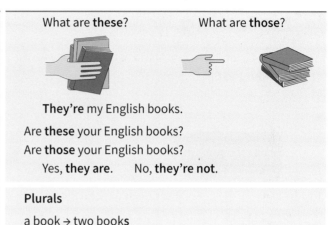

What are **these**?   What are **those**?

They're my English books.

Are **these** your English books?
Are **those** your English books?
    Yes, **they are**.   No, **they're not**.

Articles *a* and *an*	
a + consonant sound	**a b**ag
an + vowel sound	**an e**raser

Plurals

a book → two book**s**

a watch → two watch**es**

a dictionary → two dictionar**ies**

Note: *Sunglasses* and *glasses* are always plural.

A Complete the conversations with the correct words. Then practice with a partner.

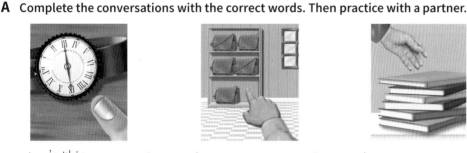

A What ___'s this___ ?
B ___It's a watch.___

A What _____ ?
B _____

A What _____ ?
B _____

A What _____ ?
B _____

B PAIR WORK Ask and answer questions about everyday items in your classroom.

4 Pronunciation Plurals

🎧 Listen and repeat. Notice that some words have an extra syllable in their plural forms.

Same syllables	Extra syllables
eraser / erasers	actress / actress·es
key / keys	address / address·es
laptop / laptops	watch / watch·es

5 Speaking In my bag

PAIR WORK Ask and answer 10 questions about the everyday items in your bags and in the classroom.

A: Is this your English book?

B: No, it's not. It's my dictionary. What are those?

A: They're my keys.

6 Keep talking!

Go to page 130 for more practice.

I can ask about and identify everyday items. ✓

B What's this called in English?

1 Listening Around the classroom

A 🎧 Listen to Bo and Marta ask about new words in English. Number the pictures from 1 to 5.

☐ an alarm clock   ☐ a map   ☐ a marker   ☐ a poster   1 a remote control

B What things in Part A are in your classroom?

2 Interactions Asking about new words

A 🎧 Listen and practice.

Alex	Excuse me. What's this called in English?
Lucy	It's a keychain.
Alex	A keychain? How do you spell that?
Lucy	K-E-Y-C-H-A-I-N.
Alex	Thanks.

B 🎧 Listen to the expressions. Then practice the conversation again with the new expressions.

Asking what something is

(What's this called in English?)   (What's the word for this in English?)   (How do you say this in English?)

C **PAIR WORK** Practice the conversation again with the things in Exercise 1.

A: Excuse me. What's this called in English?

B: It's a map.

A: How do you spell that?

3 Speaking More everyday items

A 🎧 **Listen and repeat.**

1 a camera
2 a comb
3 a hairbrush
4 a coin

5 a flash drive
6 a wallet
7 a magazine
8 a newspaper

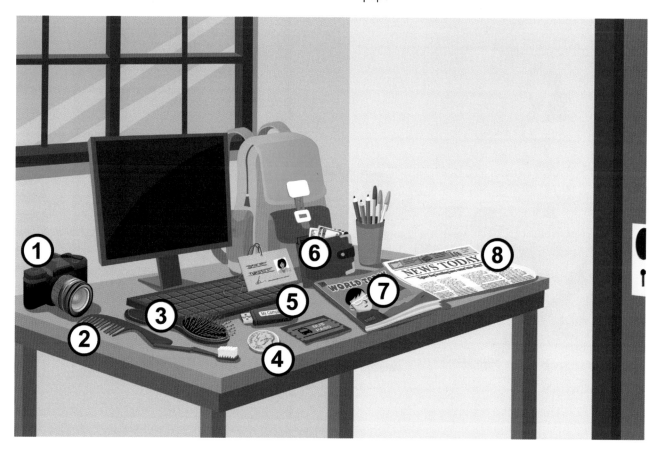

B PAIR WORK **Cover the words. What is each thing called? Answer with the information you remember.**

A: What's this called?

B: I think it's a ...

C PAIR WORK **Ask and answer questions about other things in the picture.**

A: What's the word for this in English?

B: It's a student I.D.

A: What's this called?

B: Hmm ... I don't know. Let's ask the teacher.

I can ask what something is called in English. ✅

C Clothing

1 Vocabulary Clothes and colors

A 🎧 Listen and repeat.

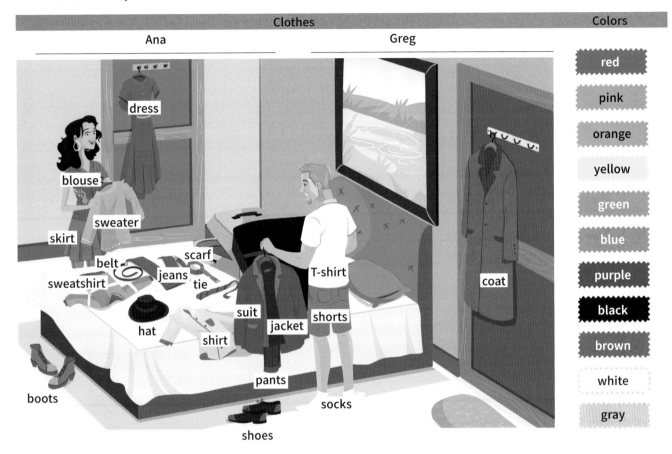

Clothes		Colors
Ana	Greg	

Ana: dress, blouse, sweater, skirt, belt, sweatshirt, scarf, jeans, tie, hat, shirt, boots, shoes

Greg: T-shirt, suit, jacket, shorts, pants, socks, coat

Colors: red, pink, orange, yellow, green, blue, purple, black, brown, white, gray

B **PAIR WORK** Describe a classmate's clothes, but don't say his or her name!
Your partner guesses the name. Take turns.

A: His shoes are brown. His T-shirt is red and green. His pants are gray.

B: Is it David?

2 Conversation Whose bag is it?

🎧 Listen and practice.

Greg	Excuse me. I think that's my bag.
Laura	This bag?
Greg	Yes, I think it's mine.
Laura	It is? Oh, yes. This bag is black and yellow. Mine is black and green. I'm very sorry.
Greg	That's OK. Is that bag yours?
Laura	Yes, thank you.
Greg	You're welcome.

3 Grammar 🎧 Possessive pronouns; *Whose*; *'s* and *s'*

It's my bag → It's **mine**.
It's your jacket. → It's **yours**.
It's his coat. → It's **his**.
They're her shoes. → They're **hers**.
They're our clothes. → They're **ours**.
It's their bag. → It's **theirs**.

Whose bag is this?
It's Greg**'s** (bag).
Whose bag is that?
It's the student**'s** (bag).
Whose bags are those?
They're the students**'** (bags).

A Circle the correct words. Then practice with a partner.

1   Whose clothes are these?   They're **your** / **our** / ⬭**ours**⬭.
2   Are these Greg's black shoes?   Yes, they're **his** / **hers** / **theirs**.
3   Is this pink scarf Ana's?   No, it's not **his** / **hers** / **theirs**.
4   Are these bags Greg and Ana's?   Yes, they're **his** / **hers** / **theirs**.
5   Whose red socks are these? Are they yours?   Yes, they're **my** / **mine** / **yours**.
6   Is that my sister's skirt?   No, it's not **mine** / **yours** / **hers**.

B 　PAIR WORK　 Ask and answer questions about the clothing in Exercise 1.

A: *Whose jeans are these?*
B: *They're Ana's. Whose T-shirt is this?*
A: *It's …*

4 Speaking Yes, it's mine.

CLASS ACTIVITY　 Put three of your things on a table. Then take three other things and find their owners.

A: *Whose hat is this?*
B: *I think it's Ken's.*
A: *Is this your hat, Ken?*
C: *Yes, it's mine.*

5 Keep talking!

Student A go to page 131 and Student B go to page 132 for more practice.

I can talk about clothes and possessions. ✓

D Favorite things

1 Reading 🎧

A Look at the things in the pictures. What are they?

B Read Yuna's blog. Circle the things you think Yuna is interested in: sports / art / fashion / movies

---

YUNA'S BLOG: MY FAVORITE THINGS!

This is my favorite photo of my grandfather. He's from Kyoto.

This T-shirt is my favorite item of clothing. It's from a street market in Mexico.

This is my favorite remote control. It's for my brother. He talks and talks and talks!

Here's a photo of my favorite umbrella. It's my little sister's. She's 8 years old.

This is my favorite painting. It's by Salvador Dalí. He's from Spain.

This backpack is my favorite. It's my friend Marisa's. It's from San Francisco.

C Read the webpage again. Answer the questions.

1 Who is from Kyoto? _Yuna's grandfather is from Kyoto._

2 Where is Yuna's T-shirt from? _____

3 Who talks a lot? _____

4 How old is Yuna's sister? _____

5 Who is Yuna's favorite painting by? _____

6 Where is Marisa's backpack from? _____

D **PAIR WORK** Think of three favorite things. Tell your partner.

"My favorite item of clothing is my blue sweatshirt."

2 Listening It's my favorite.

🎧 Listen to four people talk about their favorite things. Check (✓) the things they describe.

1 a ✓   b ☐

2 a ☐   b ☐

3 a ☐   b ☐

4 a ☐   b ☐

3 Writing and speaking My favorite thing

A Draw a picture of your favorite thing. Then answer the questions.

● What is it?

● Where is it from?

● How old is it?

● What color is it?

_____

_____

_____

_____

B Write about your favorite thing. Use the model and your answers in Part A to help you.

My Favorite Thing

My favorite thing is my bag. It's from Cuzco, Peru. I think it's three or four years old. It's purple, white, and yellow. I love it!

C **GROUP WORK** Share your drawings and your writing. Ask and answer questions for more information.

A: Here's a picture of my favorite thing.

B: What is it?

A: It's my bag.

C: Where is it from?

A: It's from Peru.

Wrap-up

1 Quick pair review

Lesson A Brainstorm!

Make a list of everyday items and the plural forms of the words.
How many do you know? You have two minutes.

Lesson B Test your partner!

Ask your partner what the things are. You have two minutes.

Student A

Student B

Lesson C Do you remember?

Look at your partner's clothes. Then close your eyes and describe them. Take turns.
You have two minutes.

Your shirt is green, and your jeans are blue. I think your socks are white.

Lesson D Find out!

What is one thing both you and your partner have in your bags or desks? Find the thing
and answer the questions. You have two minutes.

- What color is it?
- How old is it?
- Where is it from?

2 In the real world

What's in style? Find a picture of clothes in a magazine. Then write about them.

- What clothes are in the picture?
- What colors are the clothes?

Clothes in "Style Today"

The woman's sweater in the picture is blue. Her pants
are brown, and her shoes are black. Her bag is ...

4 Daily life

Warm Up

A Name the things you see in the picture. Use *That's a / an …* and *Those are …*.

B Say the colors of six things in the picture.

A Getting around

1 Vocabulary Ways of getting around

A 🎧 Listen and repeat.

drive a car

ride a bicycle / bike

ride a motorcycle

take a taxi / cab

take the bus

take the subway

take the train

walk

B 🎧 Listen to five ways of getting around. Number them from 1 to 5.

☐ a bicycle   1️⃣ a bus   ☐ a car   ☐ a motorcycle   ☐ a train

2 Language in context Going to work and school

A 🎧 Listen to Mariela describe how she and her family get to work and school. Underline the ways they get around.

I have a car. I <u>drive</u> to work. I don't take the train.

My husband doesn't drive to work. He has a bike, so he rides his bike.

My kids walk to school. They don't take the bus.

B What about you? Check (✓) the ways you get around.

☐ I drive.   ☐ I take the bus.   ☐ I ride a bike.   ☐ I walk.

3 Grammar ♦ Simple present statements

Regular verbs		Irregular verbs	
I **drive** to work.	I **don't take** the train.	*I / you / we / they*	*he / she*
You **take** a taxi.	You **don't take** the subway.	I **have** a car.	She **has** a car.
He **rides** a bike.	He **doesn't drive** to work.	You **don't have** a bike.	She **doesn't have** a bike.
She **drives**.	She **doesn't walk**.	We **go** to work.	He **goes** to work.
We **take** the train.	We **don't take** a taxi.	They **don't go** to school.	He **doesn't go** to school.
They **walk** to school.	They **don't take** the bus.		
Contractions don't = do not doesn't = does not			

A Complete the sentences with the simple present forms of the verbs. Then compare with a partner.

1 I _____*take*_____ (take) the bus to school. I _____*don't walk*_____ (not / walk).

2 Jonathan _____ (have) a car. He _____ (drive) to work.

3 My parents _____ (take) the train to work. They _____ (go) to the city.

4 My neighbor _____ (ride) a motorcycle to work.

5 Mei-li _____ (not / take) the bus. She _____ (walk).

6 We _____ (not / have) bicycles, and we _____ (not / drive).

B **PAIR WORK** Make five sentences about how your family members and friends get to school or work. Tell your partner.

A: My sister works in a big city. She takes the bus to work.

B: My best friend works in a big city, too. He doesn't take the bus. He drives.

4 Speaking I take the bus.

A Write how you get to school or work in the chart. Add extra information, such as a bus number or a train number.

	Me	Name: _____	Name: _____	Name: _____
To school				
To work				
Extra information				

B **GROUP WORK** Find out how three of your classmates get to school or work. Complete the chart with their information.

A: I take the bus to school. It's the number 16 bus. How about you?

B: I take the bus, too. I take the number 8 bus.

C **GROUP WORK** Tell another group how your classmates get to school or work.

"Daniel takes the number 8 bus to school."

5 Keep talking!

Go to page 133 for more practice.

I can describe how people get around. ✓

B What time is it?

1 Telling time

A 🎧 Listen and repeat.

It's twelve o'clock.

It's noon.
It's twelve p.m.

It's midnight.
It's twelve a.m.

It's twelve-oh-five.
It's five after twelve.

It's twelve-fifteen.
It's a quarter after twelve.

It's twelve-thirty.
It's half past twelve.

It's twelve-forty.
It's twenty to one.

It's twelve forty-five.
It's a quarter to one.

B `PAIR WORK` Say the times in two ways.

9:45   7:30   6:03   1:15   11:40.

a.m. = midnight to noon
p.m. = noon to midnight

2 Interactions Time

A 🎧 Listen and practice.

Joe   What time is it?

Mike   It's 9:15. What time is the bus?

Joe   Nine twenty. We're early.

Keisha   What's the time?

Emily   It's 9:35. What time is our class?

Keisha   It's at 9:30. We're late!

Asking the time
What time is it?   What's the time?

B `PAIR WORK` Practice the conversations again with the times below.

4:15 / 4:45   6:20 / 7:00   10:05 / 10:00   5:45 / 5:30

3 **Pronunciation** Reduction of *to*

A 🎧 **Listen and repeat. Notice how *to* is pronounced as /tə/.**

/tə/	/tə/	/tə/
It's ten to five.	It's five to two.	It's a quarter to one.

B 🎧 **Listen to the conversations. Then practice them. Reduce *to* to /tə/.**

A Is it five to one?	A Is it ten to eight?	A Is it a quarter to three?
B No, it's ten to one.	B No, it's a quarter to eight.	B No, it's twenty to three.

4 **Listening** Am I late?

A 🎧 **Listen to five conversations about time. Write the time of each thing.**

1 the movie	2 Rod's class	3 the train	4 the bus	5 Susan's class
10:00	_____	_____	_____	_____

B 🎧 **Listen again. Are the people early or late? Circle the correct answers.**

1 (early) / late   2 early / late   3 early / late   4 early / late   5 early / late

5 **Speaking** What time is … ?

A PAIR WORK **Interview your partner. Take notes.**

What time is your … ?

favorite class

lunch break

favorite TV show

_____   _____   _____

A: What time is your favorite class?

B: It's at 7:30 a.m. What time is yours?

A: Mine is at 8:00 p.m. It's this class!

B PAIR WORK **Tell another classmate about your partner's answers.**

"Ji-sung's favorite class is at 7:30 a.m."

I can ask for and tell the time. ✓

C My routine

1 Vocabulary Days of the week and routines

A 🎧 Listen and repeat.

Weekdays					The weekend	
Monday	Tuesday	Wednesday	Thursday	Friday	Saturday	Sunday

B 🎧 Listen and repeat.

| get up | drink coffee | eat breakfast | read the news | go to school |

| exercise | cook dinner | study | watch TV | go to bed |

C **PAIR WORK** What is your routine on weekdays? On weekends? Tell your partner.

"I get up and eat breakfast on weekdays. I go to school. I study ..."

2 Conversation Monday morning

🎧 Listen and practice.

Tom	It's Monday morning ... again!
Liz	Do you get up early on weekdays?
Tom	Yes, I do. I get up at 5:30 a.m.
Liz	Wow! That *is* early!
Tom	And I study all morning and afternoon.
Liz	Do you study in the evenings, too?
Tom	No, I don't. I cook dinner, exercise, and go to bed late, after midnight.
Liz	That's not good. What about on weekends?
Tom	On weekends, I sleep!

3 Grammar 🎧 Simple present *yes* / *no* questions

Do you **go** to school on Mondays?
    Yes, I **do**.   No, I **don't**.
 	
Does Liz **exercise**?
    Yes, she **does**.   No, she **doesn't**.
	Do you and your friends **watch** TV?
	    Yes, we **do**. No, we **don't**.
	
	Do your friends **study**?
	    Yes, they **do**. No, they **don't**.

A Write *yes* / *no* questions with the information below. Then compare with a partner.

1 (you / get up / 7:00) <u>Do you get up at 7:00?</u>
2 (you / read the news / every day) _____
3 (your teacher / drink coffee / in class) _____
4 (your parents / watch TV / in the evening) _____
5 (your friend / exercise / on weekends) _____
6 (you and your friends / study / after midnight) _____

B PAIR WORK Ask and answer the questions in Part A. Answer with your own information.

A: *Do you get up at 7:00?*
B: *No, I don't. I get up at 6:00 on weekdays and 9:30 on weekends.*

4 Speaking Routines

A PAIR WORK Interview your partner. Check (✓) his or her answers.

Do you ... ?	Yes	No
cook dinner on weekends	☐	☐
drink coffee after 7:00 p.m.	☐	☐
exercise every day	☐	☐
go to bed late on weekdays	☐	☐
get up early on weekdays	☐	☐
read the news in the evening	☐	☐

A: *Do you cook dinner on weekends?*
B: *No, I don't. I cook on weekdays!*

B PAIR WORK Tell another classmate about your partner's routines.

A: *Does Rita cook dinner on weekends?*
B: *No, she doesn't. She cooks on weekdays!*

🎧 **Time expressions**
on Sunday(s)
on Sunday afternoons(s)
on weekdays
on the weekend
on weekends
in the morning(s)
in the afternoon(s)
in the evening(s)
at noon / midnight
at night
before 7:00
after midnight
every day

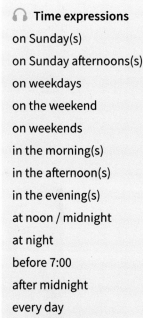

5 Keep talking!

Go to page 134 for more practice.

D My weekend

1 Reading 🎧

A Look at the forum question. What's *your* favorite day of the week? Why?

B Read the message board. Whose favorite day is on the weekend?

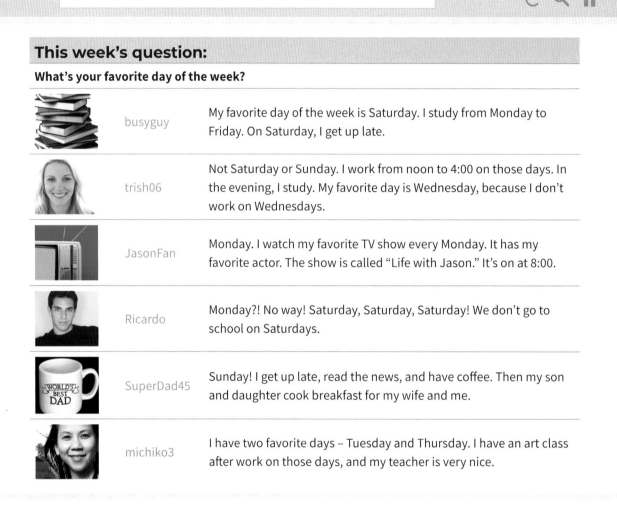

This week's question:

What's your favorite day of the week?

	busyguy	My favorite day of the week is Saturday. I study from Monday to Friday. On Saturday, I get up late.
	trish06	Not Saturday or Sunday. I work from noon to 4:00 on those days. In the evening, I study. My favorite day is Wednesday, because I don't work on Wednesdays.
	JasonFan	Monday. I watch my favorite TV show every Monday. It has my favorite actor. The show is called "Life with Jason." It's on at 8:00.
	Ricardo	Monday?! No way! Saturday, Saturday, Saturday! We don't go to school on Saturdays.
	SuperDad45	Sunday! I get up late, read the news, and have coffee. Then my son and daughter cook breakfast for my wife and me.
	michiko3	I have two favorite days – Tuesday and Thursday. I have an art class after work on those days, and my teacher is very nice.

C Read the forum again. What's each person's favorite day? Why? Complete the chart.

	Favorite day(s)	Why?
busyguy	Saturday	gets up late
trish06		
JasonFan		
Ricardo		
SuperDad45		
michiko3		

D **CLASS ACTIVITY** What's your class's favorite day? Vote and discuss your answer.

2 Listening Angela's routine

A 🎧 Listen to Angela talk about her routine on weekends. Circle the activities she does.

Saturdays		Sundays	
(work)	watch TV	get up late	exercise
go to class	go to bed late	study	cook

B 🎧 Listen again. Write one more thing Angela does on Saturdays and on Sundays.

On Saturdays: _____   On Sundays: _____

3 Writing About my weekend

A Complete the chart with information about your weekend routine. Include two activities you do and two activities you don't do.

Saturdays	Sundays
Activities I do:	Activities I do:
• _____	• _____
• _____	• _____
Activities I don't do:	Activities I don't do:
• _____	• _____
• _____	• _____

B Write about your weekend routine. Use the model and your answers in Part A to help you.

C GROUP WORK Share your writing. Ask and answer questions for more information.

My Weekend Routine

On Saturdays, I get up late and watch TV. I don't study and I don't go to work. On Sundays, …

4 Speaking Are you busy?

A Add two questions about routines to the survey. Then circle your answers.

Are you busy?	Me		You	
1 Do you study English every weekend?	Yes	No	Yes	No
2 Do you go to work on the weekend?	Yes	No	Yes	No
3 Do you get up before 7:00 on the weekend?	Yes	No	Yes	No
4 Do you exercise on the weekend?	Yes	No	Yes	No
5	Yes	No	Yes	No
6	Yes	No	Yes	No

B PAIR WORK Interview your partner. Circle his or her answers. Is your partner busy?

I can describe the things I do on weekends.   ✓

43

Wrap-up

1 Quick pair review

Lesson A Brainstorm!
Make a list of ways of getting around. How many do you know? You have one minute.

Lesson B Test your partner!
Say four different times. Can your partner write them correctly? Check his or her answers. You have two minutes.

Lesson C Guess!
Say a time and a day. Can your partner guess your routine at that time? Take turns.
You have two minutes.

A: Two o'clock on Monday.

B: Do you exercise at 2:00 on Monday?

A: No.

B: Do you study?

A: Yes.

Lesson D Find out!
What are three things both you and your partner do on weekends?
You have two minutes.

A: I exercise on Saturday mornings. How about you?

B: No, I don't. I go to bed late on Saturdays. How about you?

A: Yes, I do!

2 In the real world

What time is it around the world? Go online and find the local time in these cities.

Beijing	Cairo	Los Angeles	Rio de Janeiro	Tokyo
Buenos Aires	London	Mexico City	Sydney	Toronto

What time is it now?

It is nine o'clock in the evening in Beijing now.
In Buenos Aires, it's …

Beijing

5 Free time

Warm Up

A Look at the pictures. Make two sentences about each one.

B When do you have free time? Write the times.

	Monday	Tuesday	Wednesday	Thursday	Friday	Saturday	Sunday
a.m.							
p.m.							

A Online habits

1 Vocabulary Online activities

A 🎧 Listen and repeat.

☐ use social media

☐ check email

☐ download apps

☐ play games

☐ stream music

☐ watch videos

☐ shop online

☐ post photos

B **PAIR WORK** Check (✓) the things you do online. Then tell your partner.

"I use social media, check email, and play games. How about you?"

2 Language in context Habits survey

A 🎧 Read the survey about online habits. Circle the online activities.

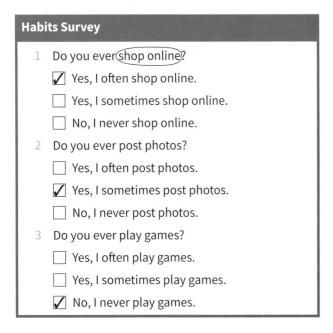

Habits Survey

1 Do you ever shop online?
  ✓ Yes, I often shop online.
  ☐ Yes, I sometimes shop online.
  ☐ No, I never shop online.

2 Do you ever post photos?
  ☐ Yes, I often post photos.
  ✓ Yes, I sometimes post photos.
  ☐ No, I never post photos.

3 Do you ever play games?
  ☐ Yes, I often play games.
  ☐ Yes, I sometimes play games.
  ✓ No, I never play games.

B What about you? Do you do the online activities in the survey?

3 Grammar 🎧 Adverbs of frequency

I	always	100%
	usually	
	often	shop online.
	sometimes	
	hardly ever	
	never	0%

Do you **ever** shop online?
　　Yes, I sometimes shop online.
　　Yes, I sometimes do.
　　No, I never shop online.
　　No, I never do.

A Rewrite the conversations with the adverbs of frequency. Then practice with a partner.

1　A　Do you watch movies online? (ever)　　*Do you ever watch movies online?*

　　B　Yes, I watch movies online. (often)

2　A　Do you check email in class? (ever)

　　B　No, I check email in class. (never)

3　A　Do you play games online? (ever)

　　B　Yes, I do. (usually)

4　A　Do you download apps? (ever)

　　B　No, I do that. (hardly ever)

B PAIR WORK Ask and answer the questions in Part A. Answer with your own information.

A: *Do you ever watch movies online?*

B: *Yes, I sometimes do.*

4 Speaking Often, sometimes, or never?

A Complete the chart with information about your online habits. Use the ideas in Exercise 1 and your own ideas.

I often …	I sometimes …	I never …

B GROUP WORK Compare your online habits.

A: *I often play games online.*

B: *Oh? I never do that.*

C: *I sometimes do.*

5 Keep talking!

Go to page 135 for more practice.

I can talk about my online habits. ✓

47

B How much is it?

1 Prices

A 🎧 Listen and repeat.

$79.00	=	seventy-nine dollars
$79.95	=	seventy-nine dollars and ninety-five cents
	OR	seventy-nine ninety-five
$379.95	=	three hundred seventy-nine dollars and ninety-five cents
	OR	three seventy-nine ninety-five

B 🎧 Listen and practice.

A: How much is this?

B: It's $54.89.

A: How much are these?

B: They're $234.99.

A: How much is that watch?

B: It's only $109.25.

C `PAIR WORK` Practice the conversations again. Say the prices in a different way.

2 Interactions At the store

A 🎧 Listen and practice.

Salesperson	Hello.
Margaret	Hi.
Salesperson	Can I help you?
Margaret	No, thanks. I'm just looking.

Salesperson	Can I help you?
Renato	Yes, please. How much is this camera?
Salesperson	It's $169.50.
Renato	Thanks.

B 🎧 Listen to the expressions. Then practice the conversations again with the new expressions.

Declining help

No, thanks. I'm just looking.   No. I'm fine, thanks.

Accepting help

Yes, please.   Yes, thanks.

3 **Pronunciation** Thirteen or thirty?

A 🎧 Listen and repeat. Notice the difference in stress in the numbers.

B 🎧 Listen to four conversations about prices. Circle the correct prices.

1 (\$14)/ \$40   3 \$17 / \$70

2 \$16 / \$60   4 \$19 / \$90

C PAIR WORK Say a number from the chart. Your partner points to it. Take turns.

Last syllable	First syllable
13 thir**teen**	30 **thir**ty
14 four**teen**	40 **for**ty
15 fif**teen**	50 **fif**ty
16 six**teen**	60 **six**ty
17 seven**teen**	70 **seven**ty
18 eigh**teen**	80 **eigh**ty
19 nine**teen**	90 **nine**ty

4 **Listening** Can I help you?

A 🎧 Listen to four conversations in a store. Check (✓) the words you hear.

1 ☑ camera   2 ☐ shirts   3 ☐ bag   4 ☐ scarf

☐ cell phone   ☐ skirt   ☐ bags   ☐ shorts

☐ laptop   ☐ T-shirt   ☐ belt   ☐ skirt

B 🎧 Listen to a salesperson offer help to four customers. Do the customers accept or decline help? Circle the correct answers.

1 (accept)/ decline   2 accept / decline   3 accept / decline   4 accept / decline

5 **Speaking** Role play

CLASS ACTIVITY Role-play the situation. Then change roles.

Group A: You are salespeople. Offer help to the customers. Answer questions about prices.

Group B: You are customers. Decline help three times. Then accept help three times and ask for the prices of three items.

$168.95

$23.99

$877.50

$400.89

$119.00

$9.25

A: Can I help you?

B: No, thanks. I'm just looking.

OR

A: Can I help you?

B: Yes, please. How much … ?

I can accept and decline help. ✓   49

C What do you do for fun?

1 Vocabulary Leisure activities and places

A 🎧 Listen and repeat.

eat out

go dancing

go shopping

hang out

play soccer

watch movies

B 🎧 Listen and repeat.

at a club

at a restaurant

at home

at the mall

at the park

C **PAIR WORK** Do you do the activities in Part A? Where? Tell your partner.

A: I watch movies at home. Do you?

B: Yes, I do. I watch movies at the mall, too.

2 Conversation In our free time

🎧 Listen and practice.

Annie   What do you do for fun, Chad?

Chad   Oh, I hang out with friends.

Annie   Yeah? Where do you hang out?

Chad   At the mall. We sometimes watch a movie or go shopping. What about you?

Annie   I play soccer in the park.

Chad   Sounds fun. Who do you play with?

Annie   My brother and his friends. Actually, we need another player. Are you interested?

Chad   Yeah!

3 Grammar 🎧 Simple present *Wh-* questions with *do*

What do you do for fun?
    I hang out.
Where do you hang out?
    At the mall.
How do you get there?
    We take the bus.
	Who do you play soccer with?
	    My brother and his friends.
	When do you usually play soccer?
	    We usually play on weekends.
	Why do you play soccer?
	    Because it's my favorite sport.

A Read the answers. Write *Wh-* questions. Then practice with a partner.

1 How do you get to class? _____ I take the bus to class.

2 _____ I eat out on Friday night.

3 _____ I play sports with my brother.

4 _____ I go shopping at the mall.

5 _____ My friends and I watch movies on Saturday.

6 _____ I sometimes study with my friends.

B **PAIR WORK** Ask and answer the questions in Part A. Answer with your own information.

A: How do you get to class?

B: I usually walk, but I sometimes take the subway.

4 Speaking Tell me more!

A **PAIR WORK** Interview your partner. Take notes.

Questions	Name: _____
1 When do you usually check your email?	
2 What time do you go to bed on Sundays?	
3 When do you chat with friends?	
4 Who do you eat out with? Where do you go?	
5 Where do you go shopping? How do you get there?	
6 What do you do for fun on weekends? Why?	

B **PAIR WORK** Tell another classmate about your partner's answers. Are any of your partners' answers the same?

A: Celia usually checks her email at night.

B: Luis checks his email at night, too.

5 Keep talking!

Go to page 136 for more practice.

I can ask and answer questions about leisure activities. ✓

D Online fun

1 Reading

A Look at the pictures in the article. What do you see?

B Read the article. What's the best title? Check (✓) the correct answer.

☐ New Websites   ☐ Chat   ☐ Fun Online Activities

Try one of these activities in your free time.

Buy and Sell

What do you want? A new video game? A new phone? What *don't* you want? Your old jeans? Your old schoolbooks? Buy and sell things online!

Where is your best friend from elementary school now? Does your friend live in your city? Search his or her name, and find your friend.

Do you have pictures or movies on your cell phone or camera? Post them! Upload your favorite photos and videos for friends.

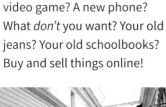

Tour a museum from your home! Go to the Egyptian Museum in Cairo, Barcelona's Picasso Museum, or Kyoto's National Museum.

Where do you want to go? Search the address and city, and find a map. Get directions to stores, parks, or a new restaurant.

Do you want to discover a new band or listen to your favorite singer on your cellphone? Use an app to stream music.

C Read the article again. Where do the headings go? Write them in the article.

Map it!   Take a Tour   Share Photos and Videos

Get Music   ✓ Buy and Sell   Find an Old Friend

D **PAIR WORK** What activities do you do online? Tell your partner.

"I hardly ever sell things online, but I sometimes buy clothes online."

2 **Listening** Four websites

A 🎧 Listen to Helena and Michael talk about the pictures on four websites.
Number the pictures from 1 to 4.

B 🎧 Listen again. Correct the false sentences.

1 Michael looks at ~~videos~~ *photos* of Stephen Curry.

2 The Museum of Modern Art is in Paris.

3 Michael shops on the website.

4 Helena often uploads videos.

3 **Writing** Let's chat!

A Choose a topic for a chat: free time, online activities, or school. Write a question about
your topic.

B GROUP WORK Send your question to the classmate on the right in a text message or on paper. Read and
answer your classmate's question. Continue to read and answer all of the questions in your group.

Sandra:	What do you do in your free time?
Jaemin:	I watch TV and play video games.
	My favorite video game is "Soccer Star."
Roberto:	I hardly ever play video games.
	I usually watch TV at night. My
	favorite show is ...

C CLASS ACTIVITY Tell the class about your chat.

4 **Speaking** My favorite website

A GROUP WORK Add a question about online habits to the list. Then ask and answer the questions.

● What's your favorite website or app?

● What other websites or apps do you usually use?

● _____

● What news websites do you read?

● What blogs do you read?

B CLASS ACTIVITY Share your information. Which websites and apps are popular?

I can discuss how I use technology. ✓

Wrap-up

1 Quick pair review

Lesson A `Brainstorm!`
Make a list of online activities. How many do you know? You have one minute.

Lesson B `Test your partner!`
Write three prices and say them to your partner. Can your partner write them correctly?
Check his or her answers. You have two minutes.

My prices		My partner's prices	
_____	_____	_____	_____
_____	_____	_____	_____

Lesson C `Find out!`
What are three activities both you and your partner do for fun? You have two minutes.

A: I play soccer for fun. Do you?

B: No, I don't play soccer. Do you go shopping for fun?

A: Yes, sometimes.

Lesson D `Do you remember?`
Complete the sentences with the correct words. You have one minute.

✓ Buy	Find	Share	Take

1 ____Buy____ and sell online.
2 _____ photos and videos.

3 _____ an old friend.
4 _____ a tour.

2 In the real world

How much are they? Find two different prices for each of these items.
Then write about them.

a belt	jeans	a small camera
a downloaded song	a laptop	an umbrella

Different Prices

A black belt is $29.99 at Style Shop.
It's $20.00 at Kelly's Accessories.
A downloaded song is …

6 Work and play

Warm Up

A Where do the people usually work?

B Do you know any of the jobs in the pictures? Do you know any other jobs?

A What does she do?

1 Vocabulary Jobs

A 🎧 Match the jobs and the people. Then listen and check your answers.

a	accountant	c	doctor	e	flight attendant	g	nurse	i	police officer	k	waitress
b	cook / chef	d	electrician	✓ f	waiter	h	pilot	j	receptionist	l	taxi driver

B **PAIR WORK** Point to people in the pictures and ask what their jobs are. Your partner says the jobs. Take turns.

A: What's his job?

B: He's a waiter.

2 Language in context At work

A 🎧 Read two job profiles. What are their jobs?

Lucia Ortega works in a hospital from 11:00 p.m. to 7:00 a.m. What does Lucia do? She's a nurse.

Henry Jenkins works in an office. He's an accountant. What company does Henry work for? He works for A1 Accountants.

B What about you? Do you have a job? What is it? What jobs do you think are interesting?

3 Grammar 🎧 Simple present *Wh-* questions with *does*

What does Lucia **do**? She's a nurse. **When does** she **work**? She works from 11:00 to 7:00.	**Where does** Henry **work**? He works in an office. **What** company **does** Henry **work** for? He works for A1 Accountants.

A Complete the conversations with the correct words. Then practice with a partner.

1 A ____What____ does your brother
    ____do____?

  B Oh, Tom's a doctor.

  A Really? _____ does he _____?

  B He works in a hospital.

2 A _____ does Sue _____?

  B On Mondays, Wednesdays, and Fridays.

  A And _____ company does she

    _____ for?

  B She works for Town Bank.

B PAIR WORK Write questions about Mr. Miller, Lisa, and Nicole. Then ask and answer them.

Mr. Miller · Lisa · Nicole

What _does Mr. Miller do_ ?

Where _____ ?

What _____ ?

When _____ ?

Where _____ ?

What company _____ ?

  A: What does Mr. Miller do?

  B: He's an English teacher.

4 Speaking People's jobs

CLASS ACTIVITY Add two jobs to the chart. Then find classmates who know people with those jobs.
Ask for more information.

Job	Classmate	Person	Extra information
chef			
nurse			
police officer			
taxi driver			

  A: Do you know a chef?

  B: Yes. My friend Marco is a chef.

  A: Where does he work?

  B: He works at Speedy Sushi.

5 Keep talking!

Go to page 137 for more practice.

Can I speak to … ?

Interactions On the phone

A Look at the pictures. Where does Michael work?

B 🎧 Listen and practice.

Michael Good morning, Quality Hotel.	**Michael** Just a minute, please. . . . Oh, I'm
Ashley Hello. Can I speak to Laura Diaz?	sorry, Ms. Diaz is busy at the moment.
Michael Who is this, please?	Ashley All right. Thank you.
Ashley It's Ashley Tillman.	

C 🎧 Listen to the expressions. Then practice the conversation again with the new expressions.

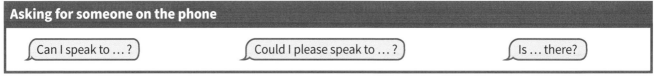

Asking for someone on the phone

Can I speak to … ?	Could I please speak to … ?	Is … there?

Having someone wait

Just a minute, please.	Hold on, please.	One moment, please.

D **PAIR WORK** Practice the conversation again with the names below.

Gabriela Garcia	Anthony Davis	Kumiko Takahashi	Roberto Santos

A: *Good morning, Quality Hotel.*

B: *Hello. Can I speak to Gabriela Garcia?*

A: *Who is this, please?*

2 **Listening** A busy woman

A 🎧 **Listen to Kevin call Star Computers on five different days. Where is Ellen Astor each day? Number the pictures from 1 to 5.**

at lunch

in a meeting

on another line

on vacation

with a customer

B 🎧 **Listen again. How does Kevin ask to speak to Ellen Astor? Number the questions from 1 to 5.**

_____ Is Ms. Astor there?

_____ Could I please speak to … ?

___1___ Can I please speak to Ellen Astor?

_____ Can I speak to Ellen Astor?

_____ Could I speak to Ms. Astor, please?

3 **Speaking** Role play

PAIR WORK **Role-play the situation. Then change roles.**

Student A: You are a receptionist at Sun Travel. Answer the phone. Tell the caller to wait, and then say why the person can't talk.

Student B: Call Sun Travel. Imagine someone you know works there. Ask to speak to the person.

A: Hello, Sun Travel.

B: Hi. Can I please speak to Jackie Miller?

A: Of course. Just a minute, please …
I'm sorry. Jackie's with a customer.

B: Oh, OK. Thanks.

I can ask for someone on the telephone. ✅

I can have someone wait. ✅

C Can you sing?

1 Vocabulary Abilities

A 🎧 Listen and repeat.

dance

draw

fix computers

paint

play the guitar

sing

speak French

swim

B PAIR WORK What things do you sometimes do? Tell your partner.

2 Conversation Top talent?

🎧 Listen and practice.

Top Talent

Host Welcome to *Top Talent*. What's your name, please?

Pamela Hello. My name is Pamela Wells.

Host Tell us, can you sing, Pamela?

Pamela No, I can't sing at all.

Host Well, can you play an instrument? The guitar? The piano?

Pamela No, I can't.

Host You can't sing and you can't play an instrument. What *can* you do, Pamela?

Pamela I can dance!

Host Great! Let's see.

3 Grammar 🎧 *Can* for ability; *and*, *but*, and *or*

I			
You			
He	**can**	dance very well.	
She	**can't**	sing at all.	
We			
They			

Can you sing?
Yes, I **can**.   No, I **can't**.
What **can** Pamela do?
     She **can** dance, **and** she **can** swim.
     She **can** dance, **but** she **can't** swim.
     She **can't** sing **or** play an instrument.

A Read the answers. Write the questions. Then practice with a partner.

1   *Can Jenny swim?* _____   No, Jenny can't swim.
2   _____   Billy can fix computers.
3   _____   Yes, Tom and Jill can sing very well.
4   _____   No, I can't play an instrument.
5   _____   Jay and I can dance and speak French.
6   _____   No, Sally can't paint at all.

B PAIR WORK Make six sentences about Frank with *and*, *but*, or *or*. Tell your partner.

Frank's Abilities

☑ draw   ☒ sing   ☑ swim
☒ paint   ☒ dance   ☑ play the guitar

"Frank can draw, but ..."

4 Pronunciation *Can* and *can't*

A 🎧 Listen and repeat. Notice the pronunciation of *can* /kən/ and *can't* /kænt/.

I can draw.   I can't paint.   I can draw, but I can't paint.

B 🎧 Listen to the conversations. Do you hear *can* or *can't*? Circle the correct answers.

1   can /(can't)   2   can / can't   3   can / can't   4   can / can't

5 Speaking *Can you paint?*

A PAIR WORK Add two abilities to the chart. Then interview your partner. Check (✓) the things he or she can do.

Can you ... ?			
paint	cook	sing in English	ride a bicycle
draw	dance	play an instrument	
swim	drive	fix a car	

B PAIR WORK Tell another classmate about your partner's abilities. Can your partner do something that you can't? What is it?

6 Keep talking!

Go to page 138 for more practice.

I can describe my talents and abilities. ✓

61

D Work and study

1 Reading 🎧

A Look at the pictures. Where are these people? Guess.

B Read the article. Which jobs include travel?

FUN JOBS

WATER SLIDE TESTER

Every new water slide needs a water slide tester! Your job: visit new water parks and be the first person down the water slide. It's fun, and you can swim every day on the job.

PANDA NANNY

A panda nanny works with baby pandas in China. Usually, you hang out and play games with pandas. You often cook dinner for them, too. Sometimes you even wear a panda suit!

CRUISE SHIP WAITER

A cruise ship waiter works in a restaurant on a ship. Your working day is long – you often work breakfast, lunch, and dinner – but you can travel to many countries and meet lots of people.

VIDEO GAME DESIGNER

A video game designer works for a software company and helps to make new video games. Usually, you are in a large team, and you work on one game for many months. Video game companies need artists, writers, and computer programmers.

C Read the article again. Answer the questions.

1 Which job has long hours?   *cruise ship waiter*
2 In which job do you work on a computer?
3 Which job is only in China?
4 In which job do you travel to many countries?
5 In which job can you swim every day?
6 In which job do you play with animals?

D **PAIR WORK** Which job is your favorite? Which job sounds hard? Can you think of other fun jobs? Tell your partner.

2 Listening Exciting opportunities

A 🎧 Listen to two students discuss three advertisements. Number them from 1 to 3.

Volunteer!

Are you interested in animals?
Can you swim? _____
with turtles in Costa Rica. Work
_____ to Saturday,
6:00 a.m. to _____ p.m.
For more information, send an email
to **CRVolunteer@cup.edu**

☐

Be an Intern

Are you 18 to _____
years old? Can you speak Chinese,
_____, Japanese, or
English? Be an intern at a theme
_____ in Hong Kong! Email
us at **hongkong@cup.com/intern**

☐

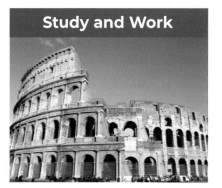
Study and Work

Can you cook? Come to Rome. Study
Italian in the morning and work in a
restaurant in the _evening_. See
the city in your _____ time!
_____ salary. Contact us at
study&work@cambridge.org

1

B 🎧 Listen again. Complete the sentences with the correct words.

3 Writing My abilities

A Make lists of things you can and can't do well. Then write a paragraph about your abilities. Use the model and your lists to help you.

My Abilities

I can play sports. I can play basketball and tennis very well. My favorite sport is soccer, but I can't play it very well. I can't play golf at all!

B **PAIR WORK** Share your paragraphs. Ask and answer questions for more information.

4 Speaking How well can you … ?

GROUP WORK Discuss the opportunities in Exercise 1, Exercise 2, or your own ideas.

- What abilities do you need in each program?
- How well can you do each thing? (very well? well? not well? not at all?)
- Are any of the programs right for you?

I can talk about study and work programs. ✓

63

Wrap-up

1 Quick pair review

Lesson A Guess!

Describe a job, but don't say what it is. Can your partner guess it? Take turns.
You have two minutes.

A: This person drives a car.

B: Is he a police officer?

A: No. The car is yellow in New York City.

B: Is he a taxi driver?

A: Yes.

Lesson B Brainstorm!

Make a list of ways to ask for someone on the phone and have someone wait.
You have two minutes.

Lesson C Find out!

What are two things both you and your partner can do? What are two things you can't do?
You have two minutes.

A: Can you cook?

B: Not really. Can you?

A: No, I can't!

Lesson D Do you remember?

Are the sentences true or false? Write *T* (true) or *F* (false). You have two minutes.

1   A water slide tester hangs out and plays games. ___F___

2   A panda nanny travels to many countries. _____

3   A cruise ship waiter meets lots of people. _____

4   A video game designer works on a ship. _____

2 In the real world

Go online and find information in English about a program in a different country. Then write about it.

● What is the name of the program?

● Where is the program?

● What kind of program is it?

● What do people do in the program?

The Peace Corps

The Peace Corps is an international program.
Americans volunteer in many countries.
They help build things and teach people.

Name circle

A **GROUP WORK** Stand in a circle. Go around the circle and say your first names. Repeat your classmates' names before you say your own name.

B **GROUP WORK** Go around the circle again. Repeat your classmates' full names.

A: My name is Eduardo Sanchez.

B: His name is Eduardo Sanchez. My name is Ming-mei Lee.

C: His name is Eduardo Sanchez. Her name is Ming-mei Lee. My name ...

Lesson C

Entertainment awards

Student A

You and your partner have pictures of the same people, but some of the jobs and cities are different. Ask questions to find the differences. Circle them.

A: Is Antonio Loren a model in your picture?

B: Yes, he is.

A: OK. That's the same. Is he from Rome?

B: No, he's from Milan. That's different.

Around the world

A Create a "new" identity. Write your new name and the country and city you are from.

Name:
Country:
City:

B **GROUP WORK** Interview four classmates. Complete the cards with their "new" identities.

Name: Country: City:	Name: Country: City:

Name: Country: City:	Name: Country: City:

A: Hi. What's your name?

B: Hi. My name is Sophie Manet.

A: Where are you from, Sophie?

B: I'm from France.

A: Oh, you're French. What city are you from?

B: I'm from Paris.

Keep talking!

127

Entertainment awards

Student B

PAIR WORK You and your partner have pictures of the same people, but some of the jobs and cities are different. Ask questions to find the differences. Circle them.

A: Is Antonio Loren a model in your picture?

B: Yes, he is.

A: OK. That's the same. Is he from Rome?

B: No, he's from Milan. That's different.

Keep talking!

Family tree

A Draw your family tree. Include your family members, their names, and their ages.

My father, Cesar

My mother, Emilia

My brother, Cesar

Me, Roberto

My wife, Claudia

Our daughter, Isabel

Our son, Ivan

My Family Tree

B PAIR WORK Tell your partner about your family tree, but don't show it! Your partner draws it on another sheet of paper. Take turns.

A: My grandfather is George. He's 72 years old. My grandmother is Anna.

B: How do you spell "Anna"?

A: A-N-N-A.

B: OK, thanks.

A: She's 68. Their kids are ...

C PAIR WORK Compare your drawing with your partner's family tree. Are they the same?

Keep talking!

Cleaning the closet

PAIR WORK Look at Dean and Lucy's closet. What things are in their closet?

A: What's that?

B: It's a dictionary. What's that?

A: It's a cell phone. Hey, what are these?

Keep talking!

What color?

Student A

A PAIR WORK You and your partner have pictures of the same people, but some of their clothes are different colors. Describe the clothing to find the differences. Circle them.

A: In my picture, Alice's coat is blue and white.

B: That's the same in mine. And her pants are gray.

A: In my picture, her pants are green. That's different.

B PAIR WORK Cover the picture. What is the same? Answer with the information you remember.

A: Alice's coat is blue and white.

B: Yes. And Ben's pants are …

Keep talking! 131

What color?

Student B

A PAIR WORK You and your partner have pictures of the same people, but some of their clothes are different colors. Describe the clothing to find the differences. Circle them.

A: In my picture, Alice's coat is blue and white.

B: That's the same in mine. And her pants are gray.

A: In my picture, her pants are green. That's different.

B PAIR WORK Cover the picture. What is the same? Answer with the information you remember.

A: Alice's coat is blue and white.

B: Yes. And Ben's pants are ...

Keep talking!

Car, train, bus, or bicycle?

A Look at the ways people get to work in Los Angeles.

How people in Los Angeles get to work	
73%	drive alone
10%	drive with others
7%	take the bus, train, or subway
3%	walk
1%	ride a bicycle
5%	work from home

Note: % = percent

B **PAIR WORK** Guess the ways people get to work in Washington, D.C. Complete the chart with the numbers. Then check your answers on the bottom of page 134.

1%	4%	5%	6%	13%	32%	39%

How people in Washington, D.C. get to work	
_____%	drive alone
_____%	drive with others
_____%	take the bus, train, or subway
_____%	walk
_____%	ride a bike
_____%	other
_____%	work from home

C **GROUP WORK** Guess the ways people get to work where *you* live. Rank them from 1 to 8.

_____ drive alone   _____ ride a bicycle   _____ take the bus, train, or subway   _____ walk

_____ drive with others   _____ take a taxi   _____ work from home   _____ other

A: I think number 1 is "take the bus, train, or subway."

B: I agree. I think number 2 is "drive alone."

Keep talking!

Routines

A **CLASS ACTIVITY** Find classmates who do each thing. Write their names.

Find someone who …	Name	Find someone who …	Name
gets up before 6:00		sleeps a lot on weekends	
studies in the morning		walks to class	
takes a shower at night		has a red bike	
has coffee at home		reads on the bus	
reads every day		takes a bath in the morning	
goes to bed early		drives a sports car	
watches TV after midnight		doesn't cook	

take a shower

study on the bus

drive a sports car

A: Do you get up before 6:00, Donna?

B: No, I don't. I get up at 6:30.

A: How about you, Michael? Do you get up before 6:00?

C: Yes, I do.

B Share your information.

A: Michael gets up before 6:00.

B: And Angela gets up before 6:00. David studies in the morning.

Answers to Keep talking! Unit 4 Lesson A, Part B (page 133): 32% drive alone; 6% drive with others; 39% take the bus, train, or subway; 13% walk; 4% ride a bike; 5% work at home; 1% other

Keep talking!

On the computer

A Add two more questions about online activities to the chart.

Do you ever … ?	Name:
read people's blogs	
buy books online	
watch movies online	
search the internet in English	
write articles or blogs	
chat with friends online	
listen to podcasts	

search the internet in English

chat with friends online

buy books online

B PAIR WORK Interview your partner. Complete the chart with his or her answers. Use adverbs of frequency.

A: Naoko, do you ever read people's blogs?

B: Oh, yes. I often do. Do you?

A: I hardly ever do.

B: Do you ever …

C PAIR WORK Tell another classmate about your partner's answers.

A: Naoko often reads people's blogs.

B: Sasha never does.

Follow-up questions

A Add two more questions about each topic to the charts.

Sports and games	Questions	Name: _____
	Do you ever play sports?	
	What do you play?	
	Who do you play with?	

Shopping	Questions	Name: _____
	Do you ever go shopping?	
	Where do you shop?	
	What do you buy there?	

Getting around	Questions	Name: _____
	Do you ever take the bus?	
	Why do you take the bus?	
	When do you take it?	

B CLASS ACTIVITY Find a classmate who does each activity. Then ask the follow-up questions. Take notes.

A: *Do you ever play sports, Samantha?*

B: *Yes, I sometimes do.*

A: *What do you play?*

B: *I play tennis.*

C Share your information. What answers are popular in your class?

Keep talking!

Job details

A Look at the picture for two minutes. Try to remember the people's names, jobs, and other information.

B PAIR WORK Cover the picture. Ask the questions and answer with the information you remember.

- What does Ana do?
- Where does she work?
- Who does she work with?
- What does Paul do?
- How does Jane get to work?

- What does Luis do?
- Where does Mei-li work?
- What does she do?
- What company does Mitch work for?
- What does Carla do?

A: What *does Ana do?*

B: I think she's *a waitress.*

A: Yes, I think so, too. Where *does she work?*

C PAIR WORK Ask and answer two more questions about the picture.

Keep talking!

Start to finish

GROUP WORK Play the game. Put a small object on *Start*. Toss a coin.

 Move 1 space.

Heads

 Move 2 spaces.

Tails

Read the question. Can you do what it says? Take turns.
Yes. → Move forward.   No. ← Move back.

START

Can you spell your first name backward?
Carlos: S-O-L-R-A-C.
← 1 space   2 spaces →

Can you whistle?
← 2 spaces   1 space →

Can you name the days of the week in English?
Monday, . . .
← 2 spaces   1 space →

Can you answer this question?
What time is it?
← 2 spaces   1 space →

Can you read music?
← 1 space   3 spaces →

Can you name eight nationalities?
← 1 space   1 space →

Can you name nine colors?
← 3 spaces   1 space →

Can you shoot a basketball?
← 1 space   2 spaces →

What can you do online? Name two things.
← 2 spaces   1 space →

Can you sing karaoke in English?
← 2 spaces   2 spaces →

Can you name eight countries in alphabetical order?
Australia, Brazil, Canada . . .
← 2 spaces   1 space →

Can you count from 1 to 20 in English?
← 2 spaces   1 space →

Can you ask for someone on the phone?
← 2 spaces   1 space →

Can you answer this question?
What's your morning routine?
← 2 spaces   2 spaces →

Can you talk about your family for one minute?
← 3 spaces   1 space →

Can you name six things in the classroom?
← 3 spaces   3 spaces →

Can you answer this question?
What do you usually do on Saturday night?
← 1 space   2 spaces →

Can you name seven ways of getting around?
← 1 space   2 spaces →

FINISH

Keep talking!

Irregular verbs

Base form	Simple past
be	was, were
become	became
build	built
buy	bought
can	could
choose	chose
come	came
do	did
draw	drew
drink	drank
drive	drove
eat	ate
fall	fell
feel	felt
fly	flew
get	got
give	gave
go	went
hang	hung
have	had
hear	heard
hold	held
know	knew
leave	left

Base form	Simple past
lose	lost
make	made
meet	met
pay	paid
read	read
ride	rode
run	ran
say	said
see	saw
sell	sold
send	sent
sing	sang
sit	sat
sleep	slept
speak	spoke
spend	spent
stand	stood
swim	swam
take	took
teach	taught
think	thought
wear	wore
win	won
write	wrote

Credits

The authors and publishers acknowledge the following sources of copyright material and are grateful for the permissions granted. While every effort has been made, it has not always been possible to identify the sources of all the material used, or to trace all copyright holders. If any omissions are brought to our notice, we will be happy to include the appropriate acknowledgements on reprinting and in the next update to the digital edition, as applicable.

Photography
All below images are sourced from Getty Images.
U1: Dougal Waters/DigitalVision; Nattakorn Maneerat/iStock/Getty Images Plus; drbimages/E+; mathiaswilson/E+; Alys Tomlinson/Cultura; kali9/E+; Gary John Norman/Blend Images; Vincent Sandoval/Getty Images Entertainment; Michael Tran/FilmMagic; Jason Merritt/Getty Images Entertainment; Kevin Winter/WireImage; Noam Galai/FilmMagic; PeopleImages/DigitalVision; ©Christa Van Den Heuvel; Jason Merritt/Getty Images Entertainment; Manuel Blondeau - Corbis/AOP Press/Corbis Sport; ©GV Cruz; Jim Spellman/WireImage; VCG/Visual China Group; ©Scott Gries; Kevin Mazur/WireImage; Victor Chavez/WireImage; Focus on Sport; Jason Merritt/TERM/Getty Images Entertainment; ©Jon Kopaloff; Ryan Pierse/Getty Images Entertainment; **U2**: miniature/DigitalVision Vectors; Marcus Chung /E+; ©Patricio Robles Gil; Caiaimage/Tom Merton/OJO+; JohnnyGreig/E+; Ronnie Kaufman/Larry Hirshowitz/Blend Images; Sami Sert/E+; Geber86/Vetta; Rob Lewine; PhotoAlto/Frederic Cirou/PhotoAlto Agency RF Collections; manaemedia/iStock/Getty Images Plus; ake1150sb/iStock/Getty Images Plus; **U3:** SeanShot/E+; Chris Craymer Limited/Stockbyte; H. Armstrong Roberts/ClassicStock/Archive Photos; Tom Kelley Archive/Retrofile RF; BeholdingEye/iStock/Getty Images Plus; koya79/iStock/Getty Images Plus; ©Istock; MihailDechev/iStock/Getty Images Plus; ©Hemera; ©E+; SKYRENDER/iStock/Getty Images Plus; Sean Justice/Photonica; gielmichal/iStock/Getty Images Plus; Cartarium/iStock/Getty Images Plus; Jerome Gorin/PhotoAlto; nipastock/iStock/Getty Images Plus; Yagi Studio/DigitalVision; maroke/iStock/Getty Images Plus; NYS444/iStock/Getty Images Plus; Eri Morita/Photodisc; Franco Origlia/Getty Images Entertainment; Images Plus; Dorling Kindersley; istock; Nikolai Sorokin; E+; ©istock; ©caimacanul/iStock/Getty Images Plus; Imagesource; creativesunday2016/iStock/Getty Images Plus; ©istock; Aire images/Moment; **U4:** Radius Images/Radius Images/Getty Images Plus; Light Thru My Lens Photography/Moment; Brent Winebrenner/Lonely Planet Images; artpipi/iStock/Getty Images Plus; microgen/iStock/Getty Images Plus; Uwe Krejci/DigitalVision; Karl Weatherly/Corbis Documentary; Education Images/Universal Images Group; miljko/E+; Fuse/Corbis; Sam Edwards/Caiaimage; Wavebreakmedia/iStock; Indeed; Peopleimages/E+; ©photodisc; ©Hero Images; ©Hemera; ©Istock; Yongyuan Dai/Stone; **U5:** iPandastudio/iStock/Getty Images Plus; monkeybusinessimages/iStock/Getty Images Plus; pictafolio/iStock/Getty Images Plus; OnstOn/iStock/Getty Images Plus; KeremYucel/iStock/Getty Images Plus; Jane_Kelly/iStock/Getty Images Plus; Madmaxer/iStock/Getty Images Plus; Geert Weggen/Aurora Photos; Westend61; JGI/Jamie Grill/Blend Images; Tetra Images; Photoplotnikov/iStock; MicrovOne/iStock; Jupiterimages/Photolibrary; Creative Crop/DigitalVision; Grzegorz Wozniak/EyeEm; rasslava/iStock/Getty Images Plus; UmbertoPantalone/iStock/Getty Images Plus; mattjeacock/iStock/Getty Images Plus; 3alexd/iStock/Getty Images Plus; valentinrussanov/E+; Morsa Images/Iconica; Boogich/E+; Ed Freeman/Stone; Danny Lehman/The Image Bank; Sam Edwards/OJO Images; golibo/iStock/Getty Images Plus; imagedepotpro/E+; ultramarinfoto/E+; Jeffrey Coolidge/Photodisc; Thomas-Soellner/iStock/Getty Images Plus; Spencer Platt/Getty Images News; Vimvertigo/iStock/Getty Images Plus; imtmphoto/iStock/Getty Images Plus; kali9/E+; Mint Images/Mint Images RF; Max shen/Moment; Westend61; Thearon W. Henderson/Getty Images Sport; Akimasa Harada/Moment Open; Tara Moore/DigitalVision; dlerick/iStock; **U6:** JohnnyGreig/E+; RUBEN RAMOS/iStock Editorial/Getty Images Plus; Digital Vision; PeopleImages/E+; ljubaphoto/iStock/Getty Images Plus; Andersen Ross/Cultura; Jenny Acheson/Iconica; Jupiterimages/The Image Bank; hjalmeida/iStock/Getty Images Plus; Wavebreak Media Ltd/Getty Images Plus; DAJ; Simon Potter/Image Source; Sven Hansche/EyeEm; LIU JIN/AFP; Steve Mason/Photodisc; PRImageFactory/iStock/Getty Images Plus; EricLatt/iStock Editorial; Owen Franken/Photolibrary; **U7:** ahirao_photo/iStock/Getty Images Plus; twomeows/Moment; Angela Schintu/EyeEm; zoranm/iStock/Getty Images Plus; Yulia_Kotina/iStock/Getty Images Plus; Jason England/EyeEm; MARIAMARTAGIMENEZ/iStock/Getty Images Plus; ©istock; ©E+/Getty Images; Wavebreakmedia/iStock/Getty Images Plus; MIXA; EricVega/iStock/Getty Images Plus; ©Hemera; Eric Audras/ONOKY; guruXOOX/iStock/Getty Images Plus; yulkapopkova/iStock/Getty Images Plus; Stockbyte; Zakharova_Natalia/iStock/Getty Images Plus; Photodisc; asbe/iStock/Getty Images Plus; Piotr Krzeslak/iStock/Getty Images Plus; rez-art/iStock/Getty Images Plus; ©Image Source; Claudia Totir/Moment; Maren Caruso/DigitalVision; SUNGSU HAN/iStock/Getty Images Plus; MargoeEdwards/iStock/Getty Images Plus; PhotoAlto/Laurence Mouton/PhotoAlto Agency RF Collections; Jupiterimages/PHOTOS.com/Getty Images Plus; Kevin Mazur/WireImage; **U8:** Willie B. Thomas/DigitalVision; guruXOOX/iStock/Getty Images Plus; ale_flamy/Moment; Jeff Greenberg/Universal Images Group; John Eder/Stone; zamrznutitonovi/iStock/Getty Images Plus; Alija/E+; csfotoimages/iStock Editorial/Getty Images Plus; Barry Winiker/The Image Bank; Joe McBride/The Image Bank; Fuse/Corbis; fotog; Wolfgang Kaehler/LightRocket; Josiah Edbrooke/iStock/Getty Images Plus; Tim Bieber/Photodisc; John Leyba/The Denver Post; John Leyba/The Denver Post; Chad Baker/Jason Reed/Ryan McVay/Photodisc; EThamPhoto/The Image Bank; DragonImages/iStock/Getty Images Plus; PhotoTalk/iStock/Getty Images Plus; andipantz/E+; Barry Winiker/The Image Bank; Alex Potemkin/E+; Thomas Barwick/Taxi; PRImageFactory/iStock/Getty Images Plus; PhotoAlto/Laurence Mouton/Getty Images; **U9:** Westend61; Chris Whitehead/Image Source; SolStock/E+; Stadtratte/iStock/Getty Images Plus; microgen/iStock/Getty Images Plus; jacoblund/iStock/Getty Images Plus; Robert Deutschman/Robert Deutschman; Wavebreakmedia/iStock/Getty Images Plus; Tom Merton/Caiaimage; Wavebreakmedia/iStock; SeventyFour/iStock/Getty Images Plus; Alija/E+; Eric Audras/ONOKY; PeopleImages/E+; JGI/Tom Grill/Blend Images; fizkes/iStock/Getty Images Plus; Image Source/Getty Images; Dougal Waters/DigitalVision; monkeybusinessimages/iStock/Getty Images Plus; drbimages/E+; schlol/E+; Qvasimodo/iStock/Getty Images Plus; John Harper/Stone; Parichat Boon-Ek/EyeEm; Peter Bannan/Moment; VStock LLC/Tanya Constantine; Mr.nutnuchit Phutsawagung/EyeEm; Ryan McVay/The Image Bank; Caiaimage/Paul Bradbury; Jose Luis Pelaez Inc/MNPhotoStudios/Blend Images; **U10:** Andreas Kuehn/DigitalVision; Klaus Vedfelt/DigitalVision; Andrea Pistolesi/Stone; Hoxton/Tom Merton/Hoxton; Photos.com/PhotoObjects.net; lewkmiller/iStock/Getty Images Plus; Wavebreakmedia/iStock/Getty Images Plus; Elke Meitzel/Cultura; Greg Hinsdale/The Image Bank; Thomas Barwick/Stone; Ryan McVay/The Image Bank; Huntstock/Getty Images; Harold M. Lambert/Archive Photos; DMEPhotography/iStock/Getty Images Plus; Aneese/iStock Editorial/Getty Images Plus; Andrew Olney/Getty Images; jarenwicklund/iStock/Getty Images Plus; bowdenimages/iStock/Getty Images Plus; MGP; Gregory Costanzo/; flashfilm/The Image Bank; Stockbyte/; Plume Creative; FluxFactory/E+; Erik Isakson/Blend Images/Getty Images Plus; BLOOMimage; **U11:** Jupiterimages/Stockbyte PhotoAlto/Ale Ventura/PhotoAlto Agency RF Collections; andresr/iStock/Getty Images Plus; PRImageFactory/iStock/Getty Images Plus; Caiaimage/Paul Bradbury; BLOOMimage; Andrey Danilovich/iStock/Getty Images Plus; Ascent Xmedia/Stone; Mark Gibson/Corbis Documentary; Glowimages; Lya_Cattel/iStock; JeanUrsula/E+; Image Source; robbie jack/Corbis Entertainment; istock/Getty Images; MangoStar_Studio/iStock/Getty Images Plus; andrej_k/iStock/Getty Images Plus; Manuel-F-O/iStock/Getty Images Plus; Andersen Ross/Blend Images; Ricky John Molloy/Photodisc; Javier Vicencio/Moment Unreleased; visualspace/iStock/Getty Images Plus; Westend61; Hector Vivas/Jam Media/LatinContent Editorial; MaRabelo/iStock/Getty Images Plus; Ferdaus Shamim/WireImage; Image Source; Ariel Skelley/DigitalVision; Oleh_Slobodeniuk/E+; theasis/iStock/Getty Images Plus; PhotoAlto/Ale Ventura/PhotoAlto Agency RF Collections; **U12:** Sam Edwards/OJO Images; Burke/Triolo Productions/The Image Bank; Stephanie Keith/Getty Images News; xavierarnau/E+; Jose Luis Pelaez Inc/Blend Images; Oliver Furrer/Stone; Shalom Rufeisen/500px/500Px; PhotoAlto/Laurence Mouton/Getty Images; Jose Luis Pelaez Inc/MNPhotoStudios/Blend Images; Westend61; GemaBlanton/iStock/Getty Images Plus; ArtMarie/E+; PhotoAlto/Ale Ventura/PhotoAlto Agency RF Collections; fotografixx/iStock/Getty Images Plus; Photo and Co/The Image Bank; Zorica Nastasic/E+; Brothers91/E+; Michael Powell/Photolibrary/Getty Images; YOSHIKAZU TSUNO/AFP; kali9/iStock; Ann Ronan Pictures/Print Collector/Hulton Archive; **End Matter:** VisionsofAmerica/Joe Sohm/Photodisc; Jeffrey Greenberg/Universal Images Group; Freelance MD-based photographer/Moment Open; hedgehog94/iStock/Getty Images Plus; -M-I-S-H-A-/iStock/Getty Images Plus; JerryPDX/iStock/Getty Images Plus; Radius Images/Getty Images Plus; pop_jop/DigitalVision Vectors; 4x6/iStock/Getty Images Plus; RichLegg/iStock/Getty Images Plus; baona/iStock/Getty Images Plus; alikemalkarasu/E+; Hemera Technologies/PhotoObjects.net/Getty Images Plus; Rawpixel/iStock/Getty Images Plus; ©Daniel Grill/Tetra; ©E+; ©imagesource; ©Tetra Images; ©istock; ©Greg Elms/StockFood Creative; ©PhotoAlto; ©Stockbyte; anna1311/iStock/Getty Images Plus; nicmifsud/iStock; McIninch/iStock/Getty Images Plus; vgajic/E+; Mikael Vaisanen/The Image Bank; iPandastudio/iStock/Getty Images Plus; Jonathan Knowles/Stone; Wavebreakmedia/iStock/Getty Images Plus; Clerkenwell/Vetta; kali9/E+; Image Source RF/DreamPictures; stockinasia/iStock Editorial; JGI/Jamie Grill/Blend Images; PeopleImages/E+; fotosipsak/iStock/Getty Images Plus; Hero Images.

Front Cover by Sergio Mendoza Hochmann/Moment; Betsie Van der Meer/DigitalVision; andresr/E+.
Back Cover by Monty Rakusen/Cultura.
The following images are sourced from other libraries:
U2: ©Joana Lopes/Shutterstock; ©RubberBall/Alamy; ©Derek Trask/Alamy; **U3:** ©Media Bakery; ©Shutterstock; Frank Veronsky; Oleksiy Maksymenko/Alamy; Squared Studios/Ocean/Corbis; ©slon1971/Shutterstock; **U4:** © Frank Veronsky; Shutterstock; Media Bakery; Pushish Images/Shutterstock; **U5:** © Frank Veronsky; ©Alex Segre/Alamy; **U6:** ©Golden Pixels/Alamy; ©Pinnacle Pictures/Media Bakery; **U7:** ©Evlakhov Valeriy/Shutterstock; ©Adrianna Williams/Corbis; ©Frank Veronsky; ©ampFotoStudio/Shutterstock; **U8:** Frank Veronsky; **U9**: Blend Images/Alamy; Ted Foxx/Alamy; **U11**: Idealink Photography/Alamy; tomas del amo/Alamy; Frank Veronsky; Ditty_about_summer/Shutterstock; IM_photo/Shutterstock; Neale Cousland/Shutterstock; **U12**: Frank Veronsky; **End Matter:** ©Judith Collins/Alamy; ©Hugh Threlfall/Alamy; ©Holger Burmeister/Alamy.

Illustration
Front Matter: Kim Johnson; John Goodwin; **U1:** Kim Johnson; QBS Learning; **U2:** Peter Ellis; QBS Learning; Dani Geremia/Beehive Illustration; **U3:** Dani Geremia/Beehive Illustration; Peter Ellis; Rob Schuster; Kim Johnson; QBS Learning; **U4:** QBS Learning; **U6:** Dani Geremia/Beehive Illustration; QBS Learning; **U8:** QBS Learning; **U9:** Szilvia Szakall/Beehive Illustration; Garry Parsons; Peter Ellis; QBS Learning; **U10–12**: QBS Learning; **End Matter:** Dani Geremia/Beehive Illustration; QBS Learning.

Dani Geremia/Beehive Illustration pp20, 26, 56, 129, 137; Szilvia Szakall/Beehive Illustration pp86, QBS Learning pp5, 16, 29, 30, 32, 33, 35, 40, 57, 59, 60, 76, 78, 79, 81, 93, 96, 99, 109, 120, 125, 126, 127, 130, 131, 132, 135,138, 141, 142, 143, 144, 146, 147, 149

Art direction, book design, and layout services: QBS Learning
Audio production: CityVox, NYC and John Marshall Media
Video production: Steadman Productions